A Piano Teacher's
Kaleidoscopic Memories

A Piano Teacher's Kaleidoscopic Memories

Jim Barnhart

Copyright © 2004 by Jim Barnhart.

Library of Congress Number:	2004093029	
ISBN :	Hardcover	1-4134-5606-5
	Softcover	1-4134-5605-7

All rights reserved. No part of this book may be reproduced or transmitted in any form or by any means, electronic or mechanical, including photocopying, recording, or by any information storage and retrieval system, without permission in writing from the copyright owner.

This book was printed in the United States of America.

To order additional copies of this book, contact:
Xlibris Corporation
1-888-795-4274
www.Xlibris.com
Orders@Xlibris.com
24894

Contents

Foreword 11
  1: Why 13
  2: Changes 15
  3: Bernstein 17
  4: Who Says You Get What You Pay For 18
  5: Nothing is Cheap These Days 19
  6: Lili Kraus 20
  7: A Great Dame 21
  8: The Dunero Boys 23
  9: Kisses From Mozart 24
10: Perfect Pitch 26
11: Hard Rock 27
12: Music: Chicken Soup For The Brain 28
13: Why They Can't Count 30
14: Music Appreciation 31
15: Competitions 33
16: You Are What You Read 35
17: To Move A Mountain 37
18: Ode To Joy 39
19: A Gegenavitch and A Nemenavitch 40
20: The Giant and The Water Sprite 42
21: Forgotten Gems 44
22: Listen To The Masters 45
23: Not All That Glitters Is Gold 47
24: Three Neglected Romantics 48
25: Truth or Fiction 50

26: America's First Super-Star 51
27: A Truly Macabre Finale 53
28: A Tragedy At Sea 54
29: King Of The Missouri Waltz 55
30: Piano Lessons: 25 Cents 57
31: It's Only A Tree 59
32: Horowitz 60
33: Rubinstein 62
34: Hats Off To Lenny 63
35: Three Fornicators 65
36: A Song For The Forgotten 67
37: Ah! New York 69
38: So! What Else Is New? 71
39: The Beloved Friend 73
40: Van Cliburn 75
41: Music As A Vocation 77
42: And The Walls Came Tumbling Down 78
43: It Ain't Just For Little Girls 80
44: Don't Put The Teacher Down For Traveling 82
45: A License Does Not A Teacher Make 84
46: Good Performers Are Crawling Out Of The Walls 86
47: Down Memory Lane 88
48: Music As An Avocation 91
49: Marian Anderson 94
50: Gospel According To Saint Fundamentalis 96
51: The Land Of Opportunity 99
52: Mimi Comes to New Guinea 101
53: Helen Scoville 103
54: Poznansky and Tchaikovsky 107
55: Dear Dr. Freud 109
56: Death of a Spokesman 111
57: Another Tragic Loss 113
58: "Listening" Makes the Difference 115
59: More on Bolet 117
60: Preparation 119
61: Competitions and Honesty 121

62: Education and Music 123
63: Another Master Laid to Rest 125
64: Three Cheers for a Non-Competitive Competition 127
65: One Dirty Old Man at The Opera 129
66: Performer Abuse 130
67: Common Courtesy 132
68: What About Those Prodigies? 133
69: Tchaikovsky and Unfounded Rumors 135
70: A Feather in Our Cap 137
71: Bush and Grant on Music 139
72: "Matchmaker" 140
73: Battles 142
74: No Time For Practice 144
75: Critics 146
76: Mistaken Identity 149
77: "Everyone, Except Me and Thee" 150
78: Two Piano in D Major (?) 152
79: More About Marian Anderson and the DAR 154
80: Leonard Bernstein 155
81: David Barber's Opera History 156
82: And, Opera in A Nutshell 157
83: Time To Let Horowitz Rest In Peace 158
84: More About Gottschalk 159
85: Olga Samaroff Stokowski 162
86: Doctor Ostwalk and Glenn Gould 164
87: Bernstein Revisited 166
88: Marc Blitzstein and The Crime of Hate 168
89: More About That Tchaikovsky Rumor 170
90: A Change For The Better 171
91: Enough. Already! 173
92: A Coda 174
92: About the Author 179

"A PIANO TEACHER'S KALEIDOSCOPIC MEMORIES" IS HEREBY DEDICATED TO:

My student and dear friend, Shirley Eng, who spent many hours correcting my grammatical and spelling errors, editing, typing and preparing this manuscript for publication. However, I take sole responsibility for any errors that may have been overlooked.

My beloved godfather, Joe Sullivan, who, having learned of my interest in music, enthusiastically encouraged me to take piano lessons.

The teachers who greatly inspired me to pursue my career as a piano teacher: Sister Mary Herman, from Our Lady of Good Counsel Grammar School, Little Rock, Arkansas; Sister Mary Pauline, from Mount Saint Mary's Academy, Little Rock, Arkansas; John L. Adams, from Little Rock Senior High School, Little Rock, Arkansas; Catherine Coleman, Earle C. Voorhies and Richard Buhlig, from the Los Angeles Conservatory of Music and Arts; Helen Scoville, from the Manhattan School of Music in New York; and, Rosina Lhevinne, from The Juilliard School in New York.

As well as the many friends and acquaintances who have encouraged me to persist in the writing of these memories: Tom Freedman, Arturo Diaz, Marilyn and Jerry Treber, June Stone, Ann Feldman, Mary Godlin, and members of the San Mateo County Branch of the Music Teachers' Association of California, including Berdine Ehrman, JoAnn Stenberg and Donald Stenberg.

To all of the above, as well as anyone I might have inadvertently overlooked, I wish to express my heartfelt and deepest gratitude.

Jim Barnhart.

FOREWORD

For many years I have, from time to time, jotted down comments about music and musicians of whom I have found interesting. At the suggestion of several of my colleagues, I have assembled a collection of these comments under the title of *A Piano Teacher's Kaleidoscopic Memories*.

While these comments may never come under the heading of literary gems, one of my colleagues from The Music Teacher's Association, JoAnn Stenberg, wrote:

"*A Piano Teacher's Kaleidoscopic Memories* is a delightful musical journey for everyone interested in the field of music. The book contains a rich blend of amusing anecdotes, short stories, observations and insights into the lives of famous musicians and composers. Skillfully written and entertaining, the book is a joy to read from beginning to end and a must for all music lovers."

Jim Barnhart

1

WHY

Many years ago when I first met Rosina Lhevinne, always known as Madam Lhevinne to her students, one of the first things she did was to take one of the compositions I was studying at the time and print the letters

"W-H-Y" on the top of that composition. Every time I hear or play that composition I am reminded of that first lesson with Madam Lhevinne.

"I think those three letters are the most important letters a teacher, as well as a student, can use," she remarked.

As the lesson proceeded she made it quite clear what she meant by that remark. The composition was an Intermezzo in B Flat Minor, Opus 117, by Johannes Brahms. As I began to play she stopped me on the second note.

"Why do you stress the first note of the second measure?" she asked. Before I had a chance to respond, she continued with more questions: "Why do you feel that the first note of a measure must always be stressed? Why, if Brahms had intended the first note of the second measure to be stressed, would he have gone to the trouble to connect the last note of the first measure to the first note of the second measure with a two-note slur? The first note of a two-note slur is always stressed, unless the composer indicates that the first note of a slur is not to be stressed."

After having motioned for me to begin again, Madam Lhevinne did not interrupt for a minute or so; but, when she did, a barrage of questions was thrown at me: "Why do you bang? Why do you hit the piano? Why do you not listen? I think you no listen. No? Why do you not make the piano sing? It is such beautiful music. No? But I think you do not make it so beautiful. No?"

WHY? WHY? WHY? At first I resented those questions; but, little by little, as the lessons went by, I began to understand the wisdom of such an approach. It seems that her idea was to get a student to listen and observe. She often stated: "I think the best teachers are those who allow the students to teach themselves. The teacher must, of course, accept the responsibility to guide, to make certain they are teaching themselves correctly and to make changes when changes are necessary."

But Madam Lhevinne was not inflexible. If one could answer a particular question with logic, she would often say: "I would not play it that way; but, it makes sense and it sounds good. If that is the way you like to play it that is the way I think you should play it."

If, however, one's answers were not logical, that student had better have been ready to make changes, unless that student was prepared to accept Madam Lhevinne's caustic remarks which might have been devastating to an extremely sensitive student.

It took many years of teaching and demonstrating to my students for me to fully comprehend the meaning of the many words of wisdom imparted to me from this pedagogical genius. To have studied with her was, no doubt, one of the richest experiences of my life and an experience for which I shall be eternally grateful.

2

CHANGES

Why are changes so difficult to make? Take Bach, for instance. Within the past few decades a whole new approach to performing many of the embellishments to the music of that great composer has surfaced. Rapid advancement in the art of reproducing copies of original manuscripts, preserved in various museums throughout Germany and elsewhere, has brought about these changes.

Consider, for example, the reversed mordent. In the early years of my conservatory training I studied the "Two Part Inventions" with Richard Buhlig. Mr. Buhlig, a former student of Leschetizky, had the reputation of a profound poetic pianist, as well as being considered an authority when it came to teaching and performing the music of Bach.

Unfortunately, Mr. Buhlig, like so many of the great pianists who were born in the late eighteen-hundreds, relied upon the traditions handed down by Carl Czerny and Franz Liszt. Mr. Buhlig, a great admirer of Ferruccio Busoni, insisted upon his students using the "Busoni Edition" of the Bach Two Part Inventions. In this edition, the reversed mordent, Mr. Busoni explained, began on the primary note, proceeded to the upper-auxiliary note and then returned to the primary note. This, of course, was to be done with lightning speed.

Now, I have been informed that the reversed mordent did not exist during the time of Bach. The symbol, which a generation of teachers and performers had mistakenly identified as a reversed mordent, was a symbol for a short trill. That trill, consisting of four notes, always began on the upper-auxiliary note.

After more than forty years of practicing those tricky reversed mordents, I had begun to think they were beginning to sound pretty good. Now, I gotta start all over?

Oy, vay!

3

BERNSTEIN

Just finished reading a biography of Lenny Bernstein. Boy! If this author is correct, Lenny was quite a sexpot.

Way back in the early days of my student years in New York there were rumors that Lenny was rather fond of young men. This author confirms that story, as well as confirms the rumor that some of his musical colleagues thought of him as a crashing bore, socially.

Well, according to this author, Lenny had no trouble exploring the private property of more than a few eager and handsome studs and a crashing bore he might have been; but, evidently, he was quite adept at making beautiful music upon the mattress, as well as upon the podium.

And, no doubt, he left an indelible mark, all for the better, for which the musical world should be proud.

In another biography it is revealed that he shared a little music upon the mattress with Aaron Copland.

4

WHO SAYS YOU GET
WHAT YOU PAY FOR

Have you walked into your favorite music store lately and discovered that the music you wanted was out of print?

Did you ever stop to think that each time you hand a student a photocopy of a sheet of music some publisher made one less sale? No doubt, the publisher is apt to paraphrase an old cliché by stating, "With friends like photocopiers, who needs enemies?"

If a particular composition does not sell enough copies, the publisher has no alternative but to stop printing that composition. What's more, prices have to be raised on the music they do print to make up for the lost sales in order to stay in business.

But the claim that some publishers make that photocopiers are the sole reason for the inflation seems to be an exaggeration. It seems to me that photocopying was a result of high prices, not the other way around. I wonder if the price of music would come down if every teacher stopped photocopying?

Reminds me of the fast food chains who post little reminders around to persuade you to help keep the prices down by cleaning up after you have finished eating. If you comply, they fire the busboy, whose service is no longer needed, and the price of the hamburger goes up anyway.

It's no wonder that we often get the feeling we can't win for losing.

5

NOTHING IS CHEAP THESE DAYS

The cost of music is not the only thing that is going up. Have you visited your local piano dealer lately?

If things keep going in the direction they are now headed, parents will have to take out a second mortgage on their home, providing they can afford a home, in order to buy a piano. Either that, or we teachers are going to have to learn to teach kids on a "Silent Keyboard."

There was a time when every family who wanted a piano had a piano. Is the time coming when only the very rich will be able to afford a piano in their homes? Are piano companies pricing themselves out of business?

In the past few years I have had any number of families whose children wanted to learn to play the piano but were unable to do so because they could not afford a piano.

Of course, the way things are going these days, perhaps it is not a question of whether or not one can afford a piano but whether or not one can afford a place to put it. Perhaps, Brigham Young saw the future when he advocated having more than one wife. The time may soon come when it will take more than one husband and more than one wife to afford to maintain a household.

6

LILI KRAUS

Silent keyboards remind me of Lili Kraus. Madam Kraus was living in Japan when World War II broke out. Although she was interned as a political prisoner by the Japanese, she managed, somehow, to convince her keepers to place a piano in her cell. No doubt, they were aware of the supreme artistry of this very great pianist.

Unfortunately, the piano had seen better days. Half the keys didn't play and those that did were dreadfully out of tune. Perhaps, her custodians, being a little more than sadistically inclined, were titillated at the sight of Madam Kraus, who, in spite of this handicap, faithfully practiced each day throughout her long years of confinement.

Anyone interested in the Mozart Sonatas would be wise to listen to the recording of these sonatas by Lili Kraus. They were, I believe, originally recorded on long playing discs; at least those are the ones I have listened to for many years. However, they are now available on compact discs.

7

A GREAT DAME

Speaking of Lili Kraus reminded me of another lady of the keyboard. While Lili Kraus was practicing in her cell another great artist was giving daily concerts in a bomb shelter in London. the public concerts were free to the public and to paraphrase the postman's slogan, "Neither rain, nor sleet nor bombs could stop Myra Hess from going on stage."

After the war was over, this great humanitarian gesture caused her to receive the official title of "Dame." Perhaps no other pianist had given so much to his or her country.

It saddens me to think that our young students will never have the opportunity to hear so many of the great romantic pianists, such as Madam Hess, of the past, except via recordings.

Incidentally, Dame Myra Hess used her music when performing. I'll never forget the little speech she made the first time I heard her in Carnegie Hall:

"I know it may seem strange for you to see me with music in front of me. I can assure you I know my pieces; but I feel more relaxed when the music is there. If I am more relaxed I think I play better. If I play better, I believe you will enjoy it better."

There was some applause and a little laughter and Dame Myra Hess looked directly into the audience, giving the impression that she was speaking to each individual member there:

"Don't you think so?" she asked, followed by a roar of applause.

And what a magnificent performance it was. More than half the audience was left in tears when she had finished. Not that her playing was maudlin. Far from it! Those tears were a spontaneous reaction to the sheer majestic rendition of the music she performed.

8

THE DUNERO BOYS

While on the subject of war and musicians, if you haven't seen the movie entitled "The Dunero Boys," you should run, not walk, to your nearest video outlet and get a copy of this delightful movie. The story is a wonderful satiric commentary on the blithering idiocy often displayed by public officials:

The authorities in London round up a number of Jewish immigrants, mistaken for German and Italian spies, and ship them off to Australia where they are placed in an encampment for the duration. When the authorities realize their mistake, life in the camp improves considerably, although the authorities refuse to admit their mistake. There are several musicians among the group of prisoners, including at least one famous concert violinist. The prisoners spend the duration of the war making music and committing one peccadillo after another.

The acting, along with the chamber music, is superb. This is a movie that will remain with you long after you have seen it. Don't miss it.

9

KISSES FROM MOZART

Speaking of movies, one of the most poignant movies I have seen in ages is "Dominick and Eugene" in which Tom Hulce plays the part of a handicapped worker. Tom Hulce, you will recall, was the star in "Amadeus." In this later picture Mr. Hulce has proven himself to be a first rate actor. To my way of thinking, this picture, the story as well as the acting, rates far superior to "Rain Man." Of course, those members of the motion picture academy know better. Look what they did for "Color Purple."

What? You say you didn't like "Amadeus?" You were appalled with the manner in which they portrayed Mozart? You think the picture tended to portray Mozart as an idiot, as well as being somewhat vulgar? Oh, come on! I doubt that that portrayal took away from the fact that Mozart was a genius and it brought his music to the attention of the general public. I think that is grounds for ample applause.

As for the vulgarity, that was, perhaps, an accurate portrayal, if, we consider references to scatology as being vulgar. One must, however, remember the times. It was quite fashionable among the aristocracy during the time of Mozart to make scatological remarks. It was not at all considered vulgar; it might have been slightly disrespectful for him to show his dissatisfaction to the Prince by bending over and emitting a loud fart; but, it would not have been considered vulgar. The Prince had probably expressed himself similarly on occasions. It would have, no doubt, been in keeping with the times. However, friends and enemies would all probably agree that Mozart was a brilliant composer who worked like a fiend; yet he was, according to all accounts, a paradigm of an arousing, carousing man whose speech was as salty as an old time sailor and his writing just as vulgar, if not more so. Take for example, and this seems so typical, his letters. To his cousin Basle he wrote " . . . I wish you pleasant dreams, go ahead and shit in your bed . . . lick your ass . . . ten thousand kisses . . . I remain forever your little Porkdick." Certainly, no man today would end a letter to his mother as Mozart did to his mother:

"A thousand kisses to you and Nanerl, and you may kiss her ass, too, if it is clean."

There are some theorists who believe that Mozart might have suffered from Gilles de la Tourette syndrome; but more than likely, as some historians believe, such language was endemic to the times. There was a time, more than likely during the Mozart era, although speaking of any form of sexually carnal knowledge was extremely frowned upon, speaking openly about bodily functions, such as defecation in the crudest manner was perfectly acceptable among even the politest of societies.

10

PERFECT PITCH

After seeing "Amadeus," one of my students asked whether or not Mozart had perfect pitch. I was unable to answer that question; but I informed that student that perfect pitch is not always an asset. Madam Lhevinne, for example, said that Joseph Lhevinne, who did have perfect pitch, often became terribly confused when he had to play on a piano that was not perfectly tuned. His fingers would automatically start searching for the right keys.

There is also another story, often told of Johannes Brahms, who, while attending a fashionable party, caused the hostess quite an embarrassment during dinner when he suddenly slammed his fist down on the table an stormed out of the palace. Later he confided to his dear friend, Joachim (Joseph Joachim—1831-1907, Hungarian Violinist), that the two ladies that had been sitting beside him were driving him insane with their chatter. 'Twasn't the chatter that bothered him so much, it was the fact that one was, according to Brahms, "Screeching in the key of D Major and the other lady, sitting on his left, was screeching in the key of D Minor."

I suppose enough of that cacophony could drive one mad.

11

HARD ROCK

Speaking of noise driving one mad, what happened to all of those studies of which one heard about a few years ago concerning "Hard Rock" which was reputed to cause deafness, as well as brain damage?

I often wonder if there is any research being done at the present time on this subject; or, has it been discontinued due to the lack of interest. Perhaps, the researchers who were involved in these studies stopped the research for lack of funds.

I believe that this is an important question which deserves a definitive answer. In a free society, I suppose, if parents want to allow their kids to shatter their eardrums or jar their brains, they have a right to do so. However, I think it only fair that they know what they are doing.

12

MUSIC: CHICKEN SOUP FOR THE BRAIN

On the subject of education, I am reminded of a pet peeve of mine: why have the secondary schools placed such little importance on music? What little studies that have been done on this subject indicated that students who seriously study music and learn to play a musical instrument do better in school. Yet, when there is the slightest reduction in funds, courses in music are often the first subjects to be dropped from the curriculum.

The news continuously points out the lack of education in our schools. On an international basis we rank far behind many countries. Particularly mentioned has been the progress made in the Japanese schools. Since the study and practice of a musical instrument is required for four or five years in Japanese schools, it is strange that our educators have made very little inquiry as to whether or not the study of music has, in fact, enabled the Japanese to do better in school than our own children here in America. Does the study of music develop the right brain, as many theorists believe, thus giving a student more power of concentration? Does the study of music lead to better comprehension? Are not these questions deserving of an answer? If there is the remotest possibility that our students' powers of concentration and understanding can be increased by the study of music, is it not the duty of our educators to inform the parents so that they might become aware of this possibility?

Perhaps it is time for parents to start demanding some answers to these questions.

Yes, I've often heard the argument that students in Japan may be receiving a far better education than students in the United States, but the suicide rate of students in Japan is increasing at an alarming rate because of the pressure. Perhaps? But maybe a lot more research needs to be done to fully understand the underlining causes of this alarming rate of suicides, if, indeed, it exists, before we place the blame on education.

Also, we must not forget that individuals who lack the ability to do a job well, and this would not exclude some of our educators, will, more often than not, grasp at any excuse available to cover-up their own failures.

13

WHY THEY CAN'T COUNT

For quite a while I have been perplexed over the fact that so many of my students seemed to find it difficult to grasp the concept that a half-note must be held for twice the length of a quarter-note, etc.

Now, I know the answer. It seems there must be a new way of teaching simple arithmetic these days. For example in an article which appeared in the San Francisco Chronicle, on November 30, 1992, one of the staff writers states that the new needles, retractable catheter needles, will cost five times as much as the old needles. These needles are needed to protect hospital workers. The cost of the new needles are, according to the staff writer, $1.50 each. The price of the old needle was only 50 cents.

Five times $.50 =$1.50.

Yeah!

14

MUSIC APPRECIATION

Since our schools are doing so very little to promote an appreciation of fine music, we private music teachers might take a look at what we are doing to remedy this situation. Often, the only source a student has from which to derive a certain amount of knowledge about the great composers and their music is through the private music teacher. Yet, sadly, we often fail to supply even a token of that knowledge. More often than not, we are too busy preparing our students for a recital or a competition to sit down with them and introduce them to compositions that are so readily available on recordings.

In some of our major cities we have classical radio stations which bring fine music to us around the clock. Unfortunately, many of our students rarely, if ever, listen to these stations. Indeed, it is a sad fact that it is not too difficult to find an advanced pianist who has only a smattering knowledge of music that was not composed for the piano. Even more shocking is the fact that so many piano students are not even aware of much literature that was composed for this instrument.

If our schools continue to ignore the importance of presenting our children with courses in Music Appreciation, isn't it about time we, as private instructors, begin to make an effort to fill this gap? By starting our own classes we will not only enable our students to become better students, the investment of our time in such classes might very well be the very stimulus needed to keep musical incentives alive for the benefit of our future musicians.

15

COMPETITIONS

Five hundred BC Chinese philosopher, Lao Tzu, said that a wise teacher does not pass out grades or give out rewards for good performance because in doing so it would create a climate of success and failure, bring competition and jealousy.

Glen Gould, who was adamantly opposed to competitions took Lao Tzu's statement a bit farther by saying that the jealousy caused by competition, on a grand scale, would bring about wars and, unless controlled, a final nuclear holocaust. Mr. Gould's hope that mankind would someday be able to live in peace without the destructive force of competition was never abandoned. He refused to participate in competitions throughout his lifetime, either as a contestant or as a judge, feeling that it would be totally immoral and intrinsically evil.

Of course, those who are in favor of competitions will rationalize that competition is a way of life and that we must accept that fact if we are to get ahead. They will tell you that competitions motivate students to practice and excel in their efforts to become skilled at whatever field they are in. In the music field teachers who participate in these competitions will be rewarded by increased prestige. Those teachers who are fortunate enough to have winners will have students beating a path to their doors as their reputations increase.

There is no doubt that we have been conditioned to compete. The question remains, however, as to whether conditioning is, by nature, always good; or as man's development improves, we must come to the conclusion that certain types of conditioning was in error. Certainly, one must no doubt agree that Stone Age man was conditioned to clobber a woman over the head and drag her into his cave. Eventually, as man's ability to reason increased it became apparent that this type of conditioning had to go through a reconditioning period in which man could find a more civilized way of getting a woman. For thousands of years, and up until only a few hundred years ago, man was conditioned to purchase that "commodity." But, finally, man reached a more enlightened stage and realized that woman was not a commodity to be purchased. Perhaps those in favor of competitions will state that the above is not an analogous statement but certainly a reasonably thinking individual must admit that it clearly focuses on the fact that conditioning, no matter over how lengthy a period, is not always to be construed as good.

Today, there are surprising numbers of psychologists and behavioral scientists who are firmly convinced that ultimately the amount of harm done by competitions far outweigh whatever good that may result from such competitions. One of the best studies done with regard to the harm that can result from competitions has been done by the author Alfie Kohn and presented in his book entitled: "No Contest, The Case Against Competition." This book should be required reading and thoroughly studied by anyone entrusted with the education of young minds.

Just perhaps it will take more effort to teach these young minds to excel in order to experience the sheer joy of personal accomplishment and that the satisfaction of knowing that a job has been well done is by far the greatest reward they can ever receive. But should not that be a wise teacher's goal?

16

YOU ARE WHAT YOU READ

I have a great admiration for fast thinkers. I'm such a slow thinker that by the time I get around to answering a question, the questioner has forgotten what the question was. It's said that the more we read, the more difficult it becomes to find one simple answer to any question. That is not my excuse; I have shelves and shelves of books, unread. In spite of my best intentions, they keep sitting there waiting to be devoured. There is no doubt, however, that the more we read and the more we study, the better we play. It is highly doubtful that a shallow mind could produce anything more than shallow music.

Madam Lhevinne often encouraged her students to read "good books," as well as books on the lives of the great composers. She often expressed her belief that we could not do justice to any composition unless we understood the social, political and historical background of the composer.

Hopefully, our young piano students and other musicians have done more reading than some of our college seniors who, in a recent survey were unable to name the author of "The Tempest." A surprisingly fifty-eight percent of nearly seven hundred college seniors who participated in that survey were unable to identify that popular classic. That same survey revealed that twenty-four percent believed that Columbus landed in the Western Hemisphere some time after 1500. In an earlier survey several college students had, when questioned about Michelangelo, responded that Michelangelo was the name of a pizza parlor.

It's often been said that we are what we eat; but I think we are also what we read. Of course, I'm certain there will be many who disagree, especially those who don't read.

17

TO MOVE A MOUNTAIN

I remember that Madam Lhevinne once said that a very diligent student could move a mountain in four years. Well, a mountain was moved on October 17, 1989. At approximately 5:04 pm on that day I had been discussing with a student about ways to practice which might improve her rhythm when we were interrupted by what sounded like the rumble of a thousand head of cattle stampeding toward us. Suddenly the furniture began to pitch back and forth; even my large Baldwin Grand's weight, I know, must weigh over a thousand pounds, began to dance on its three legs. The cacophony from rattling dishes and painful groans, which eminated from inside the walls of the house, in addition to the rumbling of the earth below us, was deafening.

My student, who had obviously gone through a series of earthquake drills at school, knew exactly what to do. She got up from the piano and headed straight to a doorway. I rushed to her side and we both stood there with our hearts palpitating furiously. When the rumbling ceased we went outside. Several of my neighbors joined us, voicing their concern and clearly expressing their fright.

None of us knew the severity of the quake and the damage it had caused until the reports from the media began to come over the air. We had been extremely fortunate, since there had been no apparent damage to our neighborhood, save a few broken pieces of porcelain.

As to be expected, as the magnitude of the damage and the loss of lives began to escalate, the usual political hype began to arrive from the nation's capitol. The Democrats expressed their desire to send aid and comfort and the Republicans criticized them for always being anxious to spend and spend; never mind that the last occupant of the White House, President Reagan, had run up quite a sizable bill. Those who know say that President Reagan not only spent more than any previous president, he spent more than all of them combined. Yet, as any nice Republican will tell you, it is the Democrats who are the big spenders.

Regardless, I believe the American people will back the government one hundred percent when it comes to helping those unfortunate souls who have been devastated by the quake.

18

ODE TO JOY

The earth may move and bridges may fall but the glorious Ninth by Beethoven that was scheduled to be played in the park was not cancelled.

Reminds me of a few years back, as I sat in my living room listening to the opening of the season by the San Francisco Symphony in which that Symphony was performed, I was thinking what a wonderful tribute it would be to the city if every household would open their windows wide, turn up the volume and fill the air with the sound of "Ode To Joy."

Regardless of the quake we have so much to be joyful about. In addition to its natural beauty, San Francisco, is, in spite of those who might hold a different notion, a city that retains the legacy of its Patron Saint: Love, compassion, and the true spirit of Judeo-Christian concept that we are our brothers' keepers.

19

GEBENAVITCH AND A NEMENAVITCH

Most of us, I think, are always inspired by an act of kindness. To witness people helping people when disaster strikes renews our faith in humanity. In the annals of music history we would probably find no better example of acts of magnanimity than those displayed by Franz Liszt.

Franz Liszt was always ready to tour the continent to raise funds for relief when disasters occurred. But Liszt's benevolent behavior was not limited to those few times when great calamities struck; he spent a good part of his life helping others. Most notable, of course, was his generosity toward his colleagues. Not only did he help struggling musicians monetarily, he gave generously of his time trying to promote the careers of those less fortunate than himself.

It would be absurd, however, for me to claim that all musicians have a propensity for generosity. Consider Richard Wagner, for example. One would find it difficult to find a more selfish and self-centered human being than that musician. Wagner had a complete lack of compassion; he was contemptuous of all mankind, and he was ruthless in his dealings with everyone with whom he came in contact, including Franz Liszt who had gone to considerable lengths to aid Wagner when he was in need. Wagner repaid that kindness by revealing his contempt for Liszt's music as well as for Liszt himself, after Wagner was no longer in need of help from Liszt. Wagner was a taker. What he could not get by command, he got by any means available to him.

Still, one must agree that he did give the world some profound music. One of the most poignant examples of giving credit to Richard Wagner was supplied by Johannes Brahms, even though Brahms detested Wagner. He often expressed his hatred for the man. He was outraged at the mere mention of his name. Yet, when Brahms received word of the death of Wagner, he laid down his baton and faced the members of the Budapest Symphony Orchestra with tears streaming down his cheeks. He announced:

"Gentlemen, today, we will rehearse no more. A genius has just died."

20

THE GIANT AND THE WATER SPRITE

When I was very young and immature I was enraptured by the music of Johannes Brahms. I was incensed when I read about Debussy's often scathing remarks concerning the music of Brahms. At the time, I was unfamiliar with much of the music of either composer; but I must confess, I had no great love for the music of Debussy. Now that I am older and, hopefully, a little wiser, as well as being fairly familiar with the bulk of the music of both composers, I have not changed my mind. I am still under the impression that the music of Brahms proves, without a shadow of a doubt, that Brahms ranks among the greatest of all composers. I have not changed my mind about the music of Debussy.

Oh, I'm rather fond of Debussy's "Suite Pour Le Piano," the "Estampes" and the "Images;" but I find the bulk of Debussy's music highly over-rated. I find much of his music much too vapid for my taste.

I know that many pianists would not agree. Some of them are always asking me, "But don't you like 'The Sunken Cathedral'?" My answer is" "No, I do not like 'The Sunken Cathedral.' I think it should have sunk with the Cathedral and remained at the bottom of the sea. I would find it difficult to name a composition which bores me more."

Of course, the statement will, I'm sure, not ingratiate me with many pianists. They're entitled to their opinions.

21

FORGOTTEN GEMS

Speaking of boring music, I am reminded of the hours upon hours students in the past spent trying to master the studies of Carl Czerny. These studies were excellent for developing finger dexterity and velocity; but a large portion of them were uninspiring. It is wise, no doubt, that teachers today do not insist that students spend so much time on these studies; there is so much musical literature that is inspiring and can deliver the same results as far as dexterity and velocity are concerned. We should not, however, forget that there are many gems among the vast amount of Czerny's compositions. Those we should not neglect.

A composer, whose piano studies have almost totally been neglected, who deserves much more attention, is Hummel. The twenty-four etudes of this composer are all gems. It is a shame that they are not brought to the attention of our more advanced students. A group of these studies, two or three, would enliven any recital. These studies have been recorded by Mary Louise Boehm. Anyone not familiar with these etudes is in for a treat if he or she can manage to get a copy of this recording.

22

LISTEN TO THE MASTERS

It is my firm conviction that students should make every effort to become as familiar with as much music that time will allow. They should do this by sight-reading, by attending recitals and concerts, and by listening to the recordings of the great masters.

However, I am, from time to time, confronted with a teacher who is opposed to having a student listen to recordings. Their opposition is usually based on the notion that it is harmful for the student to imitate. Baloney! Imitation has always been a part of the learning process. A child learns to speak by hearing others speak. Young musicians learn to play by listening to others play. If it were not for this process, progress would move at a snail's pace. If it had not been for the fact that man was capable of imitation there probably would be no music.

I once heard Madam Lhevinne express the same opinion, in pretty much the same words, but to which I remember her adding: "My dear," she said to the student. "How sad. I think, perhaps, you should find another teacher." Of course, that student had advised Madam Lhevinne that her teacher did not want her listening to recordings.

A student can get many constructive ideas by listening to various artists perform a composition. Anyone who has the fear that by listening to a recording a student will sound just like the recording artist should put that fear to rest. A student could, in all probability, listen to a recording of a Beethoven Sonata as performed by Mr. Serkin from now until doomsday and still not sound like Mr. Serkin. If, by some miracle the student should sound like that great master, he, or she, should get down on bended knees and thank his, or her, lucky stars.

Many critics are claiming that students are all beginning to sound alike today*. That is a lot of hogwash, too. Even the same pianist would find it impossible to play a selection the same way twice. The result of listening to fine recordings has been that students are striving, more and more, for perfection. Is that so bad? Today we have an ever increasing number of highly trained and skilled pianists. If critics can't distinguish one pianist from another, perhaps it is time for them to look for another job.

* These critics remind me of another story told to me by Madam Lhevinne:
" Critics often expound the theory that they can always tell when a woman plays a composition and when a man plays that same composition. A famous pianist, whose name Madam Lhevinne did not mention, once challenged that theory by playing several recordings over the radio and asking the public to write to the station as to whether they felt it was a man or a woman performing. Over 90 percent of those who wrote, including several music critics, were mistaken.

23

NOT ALL THAT GLITTERS IS GOLD

To say that a pianist is highly skilled and a well-trained technician does not imply that he, or she, is putting that technic or skill to good use. Unfortunately, we often find a pianist who has cultivated virtuosity to the exclusion of other considerations. Sometimes their playing is so cold it would instantly turn boiling water into ice. More often than not, these pianists have the personality to match their playing.

But we are fortunate that we still have many young pianists who have a brilliant technic together with a warm personality. Because of this personality they bring to us a performance of rare beauty.

These two extremes exist today; they existed in the past. Concerning pianist of the past, for example, one should listen to a recording of Tina Lerner and one by Joseph Lhevinne. Tina Lerner, who was born in Orel, Russia in 1874 could make your hair stand on end. Her speed was phenomenal. Her virtuosity unsurpassed, perhaps even to this day; but one could search in vain to find any other qualities in her playing. Lhevinne, born in Odessa in 1890, was also capable of extreme virtuosity; but his playing never failed to melt your heart at the same time he was overpowering you with his brilliance.

24

THREE NEGLECTED ROMANTICS

I previously mentioned the Etudes of Hummel as being neglected. There is so much music to learn that one would need many lifetimes to even begin to learn the complete repertoire of music for the piano. However, it is a shame that teachers often fail to introduce their students to much of the music of the composers we normally teach. The Sonatas of Beethoven are prime examples. Although there are thirty-two of these Sonatas for piano, we are constantly bombarded with a mere handful of them in our concert and recital halls. The same thing could be said of almost any composer. Mention Beethoven to a young student of the piano today and don't hold your breath waiting for that student to get any further than Fuer Elise and the Moonlight Sonata when asked to name some of the composer's piano compositions. Haydn? Scarlatti? Who's that?

Unfortunately, there are other composers whose music has been so neglected that they have become almost forgotten. Some of these composers are unknown to a vast majority of our students and teachers. There are many from the various periods in music history that could be mentioned; but, let's consider three from the Romantic Period: Niels Gade, Adolf von Henselt and Charles Henri Alkan. Although there has been a revival of interest in these three composers over the past few years, they are relatively unknown to a large percentage of our young pianists.

Schumann, Liszt and Mendelssohn were among the many composers to extol the music of Niels Gade in terms of high praise. The two sets, entitled "Aquarellens (Watercolors)" should be in the repertoire of every pianist. These short and well-constructed compositions can be easily mastered by any early advanced student of the piano. They have been recorded by the pianist, Adrian Ruiz, and are delightful to listen to.

The Etudes, as well as the Concerto for piano, by Adolf von Henselt, have, no doubt, been neglected due to the extreme virtuosity required to perform them. It is sad, however, that the Etudes, in particular, have not been introduced to a large section of our advanced students.

While browsing through a store of old and rare books I came across a book which was published in the nineteen-twenties. Flipping through the pages I found the following statement which was made by Rachmaninoff:

"As for sheer beauty, the Etudes of Adolf von Henselt rank right alongside those of Chopin."

After having listened to a recording of twelve of these Etudes as performed by Michael Ponti, I am convinced that they represent some of the most beautiful Etudes ever written for piano.

The music of Alkan has, until recently, been left to languish in obscurity; yet, he was one of the most outstanding miniaturists of the nineteenth century. Ronald Smith has recorded many of these miniatures for the piano and Michael Ponti, the pianist mentioned above, has recorded several Etudes by Alkan, including Numbers 4, 5, 6 and 7. These four Etudes, which were assigned the title of Symphony for the Piano, and bear the subtitles of Allegro moderato, Andantino, Menuet and Presto, can easily be construed as a symphony for the piano.

Anyone, musician or non-musician, who enjoys listening to fine music, should not deprive themselves of the sheer pleasure that can be derived from these three composers.

25

TRUTH OR FICTION

There is one story that has been told again and again about the death of Charles Henri Alkan which remains fascinating, in spite of the fact that it has been disputed by many historians.

Legend has it that Alkan, who had gained a considerable reputation as a virtuoso at the piano, eventually retired and spent most of his time confined to his quarters in Paris. He devoted the remainder of his life to composing music and studying the Talmud. In his mid-seventies, while reaching for the Talmud on the top shelf of a wall-to-wall bookcase, the bookcase toppled over and crushed him to death.

Truth or fiction, I think all would agree that that is certainly no way to go.

26

AMERICA'S FIRST SUPER-STAR

There is probably more fiction than truth concerning the legend of Alkan's death; but there are many stories about musicians which are not mere legends. One of these stories relates to the death of America's first great "Super-Star" and virtuoso, Louis Moreau Gottschalk.

Gottschalk was the musical sensation of his time. There are many stories told of young ladies swooning in his presence.

In the spring of 1865, Gottschalk left for a tour of the far west. After a concert in San Francisco, several girls from a fashionable girls' school in Oakland sneaked out of their dormitory late at night and went to see him at the Sheraton Palace Hotel in San Francisco. Gottschalk reprimanded them and hired a private carriage to take them back to school. Unfortunately, a scandal ensued and Gottschalk was wrongfully accused of corrupting the morals of minors.

Being a city of vigilantes, where the policy of "Hang 'em first; ask questions later" abounded, Gottschalk was advised to leave town in haste. He took the advice and caught the first available steamer to South America where he eventually contracted typhoid fever and died on December 18, 1869, at the age of forty.

Although there has been an abundance of articles and books written about Louis Moreau Gottschalk, most of them, unfortunately, are now out of print. However, in Harold C. Schonberg's "The Great Pianists," which is still available, he has written a fascinating chapter on Gottschalk entitled "The First American."

If you do not have a copy of this beautifully written book by Mr. Schonberg you should run, not walk, unless you happen to be an old timer like me whose will to run is still present but whose physical stamina to do so has long got up and gone, to your nearest book store and get a copy. Normally, I would suggest your local library, but I honestly cannot believe that anyone of sound mind who has the least bit of interest in the lives of great pianists would not want a copy of this beautifully written and informative book for their very own, once he or she has begun to read the pages therein.

Note:

This section of my Journal was written, perhaps, a few months after the Octber 17th, 1989 earthquake (see TO MOVE A MOUNTAIN, section 17. I returned to this section after several years to merely suggest that you turn to section 84 MORE ABOUT GOTTSCHALK primarily to let you know that a truly superb biography of Gottschalk entitled: *Bamboula* by S. Frederick Starr, published sometime in December of 1994 (although the date of publication in the book appears the date of 1995. I have news for Oxford University Press, New York: I purchased the book before Christmas of 1994.)

27

A TRULY MACABRE FINALE

While on the subject of the deaths of Gottschalk and that of Alkan, one of the most strange stories of all times comes to mind: The death of the Italian born composer Jean Baptiste Lully (1632-1687), a story that has been repeated again and again.

It seems as though Lully, who was a very famous musician and conductor, used to use a pointed stick to pound out the rhythm while he conducted. One day when he was conducting a rehearsal of the "Te Deum" he accidentally struck his toe with the stick. The toe became infected and would not heal. Eventually gangrene set in and he had to have his foot removed. The infection, however, kept spreading and he had to have part of his leg cut off. But the infection continued to spread and after several more operations, in which his leg was completely amputated, he died.

When one becomes cognizant of the fact that the strongest pain killer, or anesthetic, at the time was a big shot of whiskey, we can only marvel in the fact that he lasted through any of those operations.

It would be hard to imagine a more macabre ending than that.

28

A TRAGEDY AT SEA

Gottschalk was not the only composer to die after leaving the shores of America. Enrique Granados was another composer whose life came to a tragic end after having left these shores.

In spite of a morbid fear of traveling on water, Granados consented to come to New York for the first performance of his opera "Goyescas." The event was a personal triumph for Granados and President Wilson invited him to give a recital at the White House. In order to accept this invitation it was necessary for Granados to cancel his plans for his return voyage to Spain. After the performance at the White House he booked passage on the S. S. Sussex. En route the ship was torpedoed and sunk in the English Channel on March 24, 1916. Granados was rescued but when he returned to the water, in an attempt to save his wife, he drowned. He was only forty-nine years of age when this tragic twist of fate took his life.

29

KING OF THE MISSOURI WALTZ

Speaking of the White House, most of us probably remember President Truman's rendition of the Missouri Waltz; but I wonder how many know that President Truman had seriously studied the piano for several years. He was, according to several reports, quite an accomplished pianist and very knowledgeable when it came to music and musicians.

It is also now conceded by the majority, both Democrats and Republicans, that Harry S. Truman will go down in history as one of the greatest presidents to have occupied the White House.

The majority, however, did not agree with his views on price controls. What a pity! If President Truman could have had his way, we piano teachers who now find it difficult to afford a studio would not be in such a bind. Truman felt that, without controls, the time would come when only the rich would be able to afford to buy a home. Without controls, he said, the greedy would gouge the middle class to the point that they would become the poor and the poor would eventually find themselves living on the streets.

Instead of listening to President Truman, the press has continually informed us, even up to the present time, that controls deprive landlords and builders of the incentive to build by denying them of a fair profit. This, in turn, they tell us, creates a shortage of housing, thus keeping prices up. President Truman said that the public was fed this line of b.s. until they began to believe it, in spite of the fact that there was more affordable housing being constructed during the Truman years, when these controls were in effect, than under any previous administration.

Well, all over the country, most of the controls have been long taken off. Where is the surplus of housing the press assured us would come about once the controls were removed? Where are the affordable rental units that they assured us would result when the controls were taken off?

President Truman, that pianist from Missouri, expressed his belief that, when the controls were removed, the rich would get richer and the poor would get poorer.

Of course, investors will tell us that inflation is the reason for high prices. Of course it is. But, where does inflation come from? Had these investors not continually raised the cost of building to inflate their own pockets, there would be no need for the high cost of labor or material. Inflation does not trickle down from the top; it starts at the top and flows like a torrent until it hits the lowest man on the totem pole. It is only logical that when an investor increases profits tenfold the cost of everything else will rise. Eventually, those at the bottom of the market will be squeezed out.

It's time for another piano player in the White House.

30

PIANO LESSONS: 25 CENTS

When it comes to elections, I have long ceased to look for logic. When I was very young, there was a constant parade of the unemployed and destitute knocking on our back door begging for work and a little food. The campaign promises that had been made by the Republican, who was then in the White House, had come to naught. Very few people had the jobs, the money, two chickens in every pot, and a car in every garage, which Mr. Hoover promised. Tens of thousands did, however, move into affordable houses - houses that were constructed of wooden crates and placed down by the railroad tracks.

But, of course, things were cheap then. You could get any number of things for twenty-five cents, including a haircut or a piano lesson. In fact, bread was only ten cents a loaf. The problem was that nobody had ten cents and piano teachers often had to give lessons on an "I'll pay you next week" basis. Sometimes they got paid and sometimes they didn't.

Well, along came the Democrats and people went back to work. They bought their cars and they had two chickens in the pot. They moved to the suburbs, where they bought bigger and better homes, and decorated them to match the pictures on

"Better Homes and Gardens." They managed to give their children piano lessons at a dollar a lesson. They put a little in the bank for a rainy day. Everything was coming up rosy pink. So, they became Republicans. That's logic?

31

IT'S ONLY A TREE

A friend advised me that I shouldn't be too hard on the Republicans. "After all," he said. "They did include several classical musicians when making up the roster for performances at the White House, including Vladimir Horowitz."

That they did, as well as damn near convincing the country that a tree is only a tree and that greed is a virtue.

32

HOROWITZ

Strange that we should mention Horowitz at that time. I now learn that it was at approximately that same day that he died.

I'll confess that I was not a great admirer of Mr. Horowitz. Although he had a colossal technique and was capable of exquisitely beautiful playing, I felt that, more often than not, he used that technique to dazzle his audiences. I found his playing rather dry and cold. I think his performance at the White House proved my point. The whole performance seemed to say, at least to my way of thinking, "Look at me! See what I can do." Of course, that's not bad if the performer adds the additional ingredient of: "Listen to the beautiful music the composer had given us."

Horowitz's performance upon his return to Moscow, after that long, long period of being away, was, however, one of the most beautiful and heart-rending performances I have ever heard.

I think Horowitz fully realized that a mere show of technique, without giving the composer his due, would not impress his fellow countrymen.

But, perhaps, I am being unfair. I have never heard Horowitz live; his recordings had never impressed me enough that I would stand in line for twenty-four hours in order to purchase a ticket to one of his rare live performances. Furthermore, when I had the opportunity to speak to some admirers of Horowitz, I was not pleased with what they had to say. They raved about his technique. They were overwhelmed by his speed. They seemed to have been mesmerized by his insane, dynamic effects. I don't recall anyone ever mentioning leaving a Horowitz recital with their heart overflowing with the warmth and love for the music.

No doubt, much of my attitude towards Horowitz had been influenced by Madame Lhevinne. I think she admired Mr. Horowitz for his business sense, but I do not think she cared even the slightest for the way he performed. I recall that she once mentioned the Tchaikowsky, meaning and referring to the Horowitz recording of the now-famous first concerto, is not a Czerny exercise. No doubt she preferred a much more romantic style of playing. Of course, I could not agree with her more.

33

RUBINSTEIN

When the name of Horowitz is mentioned, it seems almost inevitable that the name of Rubinstein will follow, in spite of the fact that the two had very little in common. Artur Rubinstein did not possess the technic of a Horowitz. Indeed, he could be, and often was, far from note-perfect; but his playing was always embued with a sense of warmth. Unlike Horowitz, of whom it has been said, was in love with himself, Rubinstein was in love with love, and he was generous with that love. It reflected in his playing, whether he was playing the piano or with a casual acquaintance he happened to encounter on a concert tour.

At a recital Horowitz could, and often did, boggle the mind from the sight of fleeting fingers; Rubinstein never failed to inflame the hearts and souls of his audiences.

But it was not only their playing that separated these two artists. It has been said, by intimates of the two, that an evening with Rubinstein was a heart-warming experience; an evening with Horowitz was an evening spent with a colossal bore.

Still, it cannot be denied that they both fulfilled a need and the audiences of each adored them.

Some like it hot; some like it cold.

34

HATS OFF TO LENNY

In spite of my remarks, after having read a biography of Leonard Bernstein, my hat goes off to him for informing the President that he would not accept the National Medal of Arts awarded to him, since the National Endowment for the Arts had cancelled a grant to an art exhibit wherein the proceeds would benefit victims of AIDS.

Actually, of course, the chair of the National Endowment for the Arts reversed himself after much flack from people with more open minds than the pea brains who influenced him to cancel the grant in the first place. The press had previously reported that the earlier cancellation was, at least partially, due to derogatory references made to a powerful churchman.

I do not know what that particular churchman's stand is concerning AIDS but one should certainly hope that it would reveal more enlightenment than the group of Bishops who recently ruled that the education of our children concerning the prevention of AIDS should not contain any references to the use of a condom. This narrow view, often espoused by both Catholic and Protestant clergy, never ceases to astonish people of sound minds. One can only conclude that these gentlemen of the cloth would prefer our youngsters die of AIDS rather than risk the possibility of the promiscuity they feel will result from informing these youngsters of the advantage of using a condom. They seem to ignore the fact that a condom would help to prevent many pregnancies and it might also prevent them from losing their lives because of AIDS.

No one, I believe, would deny these men of the cloth the right to proclaim that fornication outside marriage is immoral; although there are probably many who would disagree with that concept. Yet, one must wonder just how moral it is to deny the knowledge that the use of a condom might save a life, particularly to young teenagers who will, more than likely, sow their wild oats, in spite of all the admonitions from these Bishops.

I certainly would not like to be one of these men of the cloth when the final Judge presents them with a list of all the teenagers they could have saved had they not been so narrow-minded.

Yet, I cannot help feeling that those misinformed clergymen are not nearly so close to having their souls condemned as are those hate-filled monsters from the far right who, in the name of Christianity, proclaim their hate as they travel throughout the country proclaiming, via their signs: "God hates fags," "AIDS is God's answer to homosexuals." One minister from Kansas was the proud bearer of a sign declaring "Thank God for AIDS" during a Gay Pride week march in San Francisco.

Again, those whose views against homosexuals are narrowly focused on the Bible's words and claim to accept those words literally, pick and choose the passages that support their prejudices. Do these believers eat lobsters, wear cotton and polyester blend shirts, allow their wives to correct them? The Bible is quite clear about these matters. Just perhaps, if these people would realize just how far away they are from actually following the dictates of the Bible they would not be so anxious to cast the first stone.

35

THREE FORNICATORS

Speaking of fornicating outside the marriage bed, several musicians come to mind; but, I suppose, if I had to name three of the greats, I would have to say Beethoven, Liszt and Tchaikowsky.

We all know that Beethoven had what is often euphemistically referred to as a social disease, which he, no doubt, contracted after having paid one too many social calls to his favorite brothel. Tchaikowsky was a male copulator. We really don't know much about his surreptitious affairs, since very little has been written about those encounters. Liszt, being the religious man that he was, would probably have preferred us to believe that his associations with his mistresses were purely social. However, the fact that Blandine, Cosima and Daniel arrived upon the scene was proof that something more than a platonic relationship was taking place when he and Marie d'Augoult were between the sheets.

Such escapades have always been condemned by the clergy, in spite of the fact that they, themselves, have had plenty of action along that line, all the way from the time of the castratti, whose duties were not always solely dedicated to that of being just choirboys, up to the time of Swaggart and Bakker.

Indeed, the clergy has been, down through the ages, all too eager to condemn those things that came naturally. And those who roar the loudest about the sins of the flesh are often the ones who perpetually seem to be involved in a clandestine search for a bite from the apple of paradise. While they warn the members of their congregations that the wage of sin is hell, they justify their own behavior by rationalizing, as did the Dama de Noche who shrugged her shoulders and declared, "If it's so wrong, why did God make it so good?"

Isn't it about time that someone reminded these gentlemen that the Good Lord has consistently shown love and compassion for the sinner; whereas He has shown nothing but contempt, disgust and revulsion for the hypocrite.

And, if you're interested in trying to figure out who, among the Liszt crowd, was doing what to whom, consider this: the great conductor, Hans Von Bulow, was married to Cosima Liszt, the illegitimate daughter of Franz Liszt and Countess Marie D'Augoult, who left her husband to live with Franz. Cosima, eventually left Hans and ran away with Richard Wagner. Matters became even more complicated when we learn that Franz eventually left Marie to live with Princess Carolyne Sayn-Wittgenstein, who, herself, had run away from her husband in Russia in order to live with Franz in Weimer. To make it even worse trying to recall who was who, Carolyn brought her daughter, another Marie, with her.

Incidentally, before Wagner ran away with Cosima, he was married to a singer from a small opera company in Madgeburg by the name of Minna Planer. I've been unable to find out what happened to Minna. Perhaps she took off with the housekeeper?

36

A SONG FOR THE FORGOTTEN

Last summer, a friend of mine visited me from New York. While he was here, we spend one Saturday visiting his elderly sister who happened to be in a convalescent home, recuperating from an operation.

The home was well maintained, efficiently staffed and expensive. There was a beautiful grand piano in the recreation room and Tom, my friend of more than forty years, sat down to try it out. Tom has a particular gift for improvising on the piano. As he began to play, a few patients drifted toward the piano in their wheel chairs. Before long, the whole room was filled with patients as they rolled in. I don't believe I have ever seen a more receptive audience. It was a heart-warming experience to see the sight of so many of these elderly people as their faces began to light up, no doubt, from pleasant memories, as Tom played Broadway hit tunes from the twenties, thirties and forties. Several of the patients requested special songs and as Tom played them, these patients sang along.

A good many of the patients were in their late eighties or early nineties, but they could still manage to carry a tune, although many of the voices were weak. Surprisingly, some of the patients who had suffered strokes and were not able to talk, were able to hum these melodies.

Even more surprising, as well as uplifting, was that one of these patients sang many of those songs, solo, and without missing a word, in spite of the fact that, we had been informed, this young lady, in her eighties, was no longer able, due to a memory failure, to speak even a simple short sentence coherently.

As I said, it was a heart-warming experience; but, I was saddened and still remain inwardly depressed from the realization, that most of these people, although well taken care of, would, in all probability, spend the rest of their days confined to their wheel chairs inside the walls of this home. Still more depressing is being aware that so many of our elderly are placed in homes not nearly so well maintained as this home is. So many are languishing in homes where they have long been forgotten by friends, as well as relatives.

What a shame the world is not enriched with a "Tom" for each of these homes, where he could spend a few hours each week rewarding these forgotten souls with a song or two, perhaps, brightening their lives, if only for a moment, by bringing back pleasant memories.

37

AH! NEW YORK

I often think of my friends in New York. A good many of them are musicians. As the song goes, "It's a wonderful town." The winters can freeze the balls off a brass monkey; the summers are unbearable; but, it's alive.

New York is not a place to visit; it's a place to live. Take it from one who lived there for over twenty-five years. If you've never lived in New York, you haven't lived. If you've ever wondered what it would feel like to be a sardine in a fully packed can, take a ride on any train out of Times Square at the rush hour and you'll know.

Have you ever accidentally bumped into another pedestrian on the street, and after having begged his or her pardon, been told to either "Drop dead!" or "Why don't you watch where the fuck you're going!"? If you haven't, you have probably never lived in New York.

If you've gone to your friendly neighborhood store where it's packed with browsers and heard the proprietor shouting, "If you're not buying, get out!" you've lived in New York.

If you've ever been taken from the airport by cab to Manhattan via Brooklyn, the Bronx, New Jersey and Staten Island, you're no New Yorker and you've been taken for a ride.

If you've ever lived in an apartment where it was five degrees below zero outside and ten degrees below inside and your landlord thought he was being overly generous by letting the steam radiators heat up for ten minutes in the morning and ten minutes in the evening, you have probably lived in New York.

If, the last time you bent over to retrieve a dropped package for a little old lady, whose arms were ladened with packages, and she started shouting, "Help! Police! Thief! That's my package," you were in New York.

If you've ever stood on a corner on a cold and rainy night trying to hail a cab and fifteen empty cabs, with "on duty" signs clearly lit up, passed you by before one stopped for you, you were in New York.

If you just walked twenty blocks and tried eighteen public pay telephones before you finally found one that worked, you are in New York.

If, by some unfortunate circumstances, you do own a car in New York and remember where you parked it, consider yourself lucky.

If you wouldn't dare enter Central Park after dark, you're a wise New Yorker.

Still, New York is a wonderful town. Where else could you find a broom closet that has been converted into a three-bedroom apartment and renting for the price of a mansion?

38

SO! WHAT ELSE IS NEW?

What an injustice it would be for me to speak of New York without talking about music. Is there any doubt that Manhattan remains the mecca for music students from all over the world? There are probably more musicians, and would-be musicians, in one square block of Manhattan than you would find in most cities throughout the United States. Students from all over flock to New York to study and to seek to be recognized as concert artists. Unfortunately, only a small percentage of those will ever get that recognition. Not that many of them lack the talent; but the competition is fierce and standards are high.

Reminds me of a student who had mastered one of the most difficult compositions ever composed for the piano. This student, who happened to live on the West Coast, was encouraged to tape a performance of this selection and send it to an agent in New York. Surely, these West Coasters felt, such playing would, without a doubt, make a big impression on the agent. Within a few weeks, however, the agent returned the tape with the reply:

"So! What else is new?"

Still, there is probably no other place better than New York for a young student whose ambition is to become a fine musician. If a student is willing to study and work hard that student will find ample rewards in New York. These rewards will, more than likely, not be of any monetary value; but the student will receive much encouragement and appreciation from fellow musicians. For a struggling musician this is very important. Of course, there will always be cynics who will remind you that that type of reward, plus a dollar-fifty will get you a slice of toast and a cup of coffee.* Pay no heed. The world is full of people who will tell you that life is not worth the struggle. What these sad creatures have forgotten, or never learned, is that the struggle is what makes life worth living. Instead, take heart from the story of the old Monk who had been asked what he would do if he knew his life would come to an end tomorrow. He replied: "I'd go right on hoeing my garden."

What better advice could be given to a musician than to remind him, or her, to keep on practicing?

* Actually, the popular quote from a New Yorker was, for many years: "That and ten cents will get you on the subway." But inflation has put that quote to rest.

39

THE BELOVED FRIEND

For many decades, when anyone throughout the country thought of New York, if they were at all musically inclined, they thought of Carnegie Hall. that venerable institution has played a central role in American culture ever since its inaugural concert which was conducted by Peter Tchaikovsky on May 5, 1891.

But if one were playing a game of word association, the mention of the name of Tchaikovsky would be equivalent to hitting the jackpot in Reno or Las Vegas: Nutcracker, Swan Lake, Romeo and Juliet. None but the Lonely Heart, Competition, Moscow, Van Cliburn, Ticker-Tape Parade, Wall Street . . . goodness! One could go on forever.

When I think of Tchaikovsky I think of Catherine Drinker Bowen. She stands out in my mind as one of the finest storytellers to have ever put words on paper. Certainly, her "Beloved Friend" is one of the most insightful, as well as compassionate, accounts ever to have been written about the life of Tchaikovsky.* The beloved friend, of course, was Nadeshda von Meck. That love affair was, perhaps, one of the most curious love stories of all times. If my memory serves me correctly, I believe it lasted for nearly fifteen years. Rather remarkable, I think, when one considers the fact that the two never met. The affair was carried on solely through correspondence.

In my dictionary Platonic Love is defined as a close relationship between two persons in which sexual desire has been suppressed or sublimated. Well, I guess the relationship between Tchaikovsky and Nadeshda von Meck was about a Platonic as one could get.

Although these two lovebirds poured their hearts and souls out to each other in their letters, no one knows whether or not Tchaikovsky's true natural bent was ever revealed to her. More than likely she had her suspicions; but, then again, she had her husband and children to comfort her. One would gather, however, that she received very little comfort from her husband.

As I said, it was a curious affair.

Note:

Once again I found myself having to turn back the pages of this Journal in order to correct this statement. Although Bowen's book "Beloved Friend" still stands out in my mind as one of the most beautiful biographies to ever have been written about the life of Tchaikovsky, Alexander Poznansky has now come up with a biography "Tschaikovsky, the Quest for the Inner Man" (see section 54 of this Journal) which will, I believe, go down in history as one of the most comprehensive and definitive biographies ever to have been written about this composer.

40

VAN CLIBURN

On several occasions in the past few years, I mentioned the name of Van Cliburn to some of my students and they asked, "Who is Van Cliburn?"

How soon we forget! for more than a couple of decades, beginning in the late fifties, the name of Van Cliburn was a household word, the name of an American hero. On the 13th of April in 1958, every newsroom in the country was screaming for all the information they could get on the background of Van Cliburn. In spite of the fact that Van Cliburn had won many prestigious awards throughout the country, he was a relatively unknown pianist to the majority of Americans. Then, on that day in April, he was, as if by magic, catapulted to a height of world fame. This tall, lanky American from Kilgore, Texas, had, with his two hands, "conquered Russia."

Van Cliburn had won first prize at the Tchaikovsky International Piano and Violin Competition which had been held in Moscow. Not only had he "beat" the Russians, he had won their hearts. Telephotos showed Krushechev giving him the bear hub. He was inundated with flowers and paid homage to by Russia's sovereign musicians. Wherever he played, Moscow, Leningrad, Minsk, Kiev, the streets, hotels and concert halls were packed with Russians anxious to hear him.

By the time Van Cliburn reached American shores, a few days later, every concert hall from coast to coast was pleading for him to come and play. New York City honored him with a ticker-tape parade up Broadway. Some news reports stated that his welcome home was the most explosive, emotionally, since the day of the Lindbergh triumph. He was a "National Hero." Pianists and piano teachers throughout the country reveled in his glory.

Yet, had it not been for the insistence of Madam Rosina Lhevinne, Van Cliburn probably would have never gone to Russia to compete. When Madame Lhevinne had first decided that Van Cliburn should go, nearly everyone she confronted about sending him felt that it was a hopeless cause. "The Russians will never permit an American to win. The over-whelming majority of the judges are Russians. There isn't the slightest chance that they are going to cast their vote for an unknown from Texas," they said.

But Van Cliburn had studied with Madam Lhevinne at Juilliard and Madam Lhevinne knew her pupil. And, in spite of the fact that Madame Lhevinne had been an American for a good part of a half-century, she had grown up in Russia, she had gone to school in Russia. She had studied at the Moscow Conservatory. She, herself, had won the Gold Medal award when she was only fifteen years of age. She had every bit of faith that Van Cliburn could win, and, of course, he did not disappoint her.

41

MUSIC AS A VOCATION

When I was studying with Madam Lhevinne, she often expressed her concern that all too many young pianists were being trained for a career in music. As she was well aware, the number of students who will become professionals is minute compared to the number of students who seek to accomplish that goal. While she felt very strongly about young students receiving the very best training, she was very much in favor of teachers placing more stress on music as an avocation.

Having said that, let's consider the student who expresses a desire to study music as a vocation. First of all, that student must be made aware of the limited possibilities as a concert pianist. He, or she, must understand that there is no room for mediocrity. Anyone desiring a concert career must spend many, many hours each day toward building and perfecting a repertoire.

Again, quoting Madam Lhevinne: "One must be a slave to the piano and to music. One must be fully aware that they would not be happy in any other field. Only then should one even consider music as a career."

42

AND THE WALLS CAME TUMBLING DOWN

Yesterday was Christmas Day. Once again that glorious symphony of Ludwig van Beethoven, in which the words of Schiller ring out proclaiming that "Joy is the bright spark of divinity under whose gentle wings all men become brothers," was presented to celebrate the breaking down of the barriers between the East and West Berlin. The performance, which took place in East Berlin, was under the direction of Leonard Bernstein.

There will be, no doubt, those who will object to Bernstein's decision to conduct this performance on German soil. It reminds me of the first time I heard Walter Gieseking perform at Carnegie Hall. The objection, of course, came as a result of Gieseking having remained in Germany during the Hitler era. Many said that he was a Nazi, or at least a Nazi sympathizer. Others claimed that Gieseking was apolitical and had simply remained in Germany because he was a German. By the time he realized what was happening in Germany it was too late to protest and impossible to leave. That, of course, evokes the question of whether one should remain silent when his country enters into a conflict, once one decided his country is wrong; or, should he speak out and risk his own neck? Such questions are not easily answered.

Anyway, the war had been over for more than half a decade when Gieseking performed at Carnegie Hall; yet, there was a strong resentment amongst many New Yorkers for him to be allowed to perform. I do not recall whether or not there were any actual threats; but I do remember that there was a great deal of apprehension concerning the possibility of violence. The streets surrounding Carnegie Hall were roped off and Mounted Patrolmen from New York City Police Department circled the entire block. Foot Patrolmen were also strategically stationed inside the hall in anticipation of any disruptive or violent demonstrations that might ensue. Fortunately, no demonstrations occurred.

Perhaps, we shall never know where Gieseking stood politically; but one thing is certain, critics and musicians from around the world acclaim that he was one of the most phenomenally gifted pianist of this century.

I consider it a great privilege to have heard him. In fact, more than forty years has passed since that performance; yet, his exquisite rendition of that most difficult trill which comes in the last movement of Beethoven's Opus 109 Sonata remains as one of the most spectacular performances I have ever witnessed.

43

IT AIN'T JUST FOR LITTLE GIRLS

Van Cliburn's victory in Russia brought about many changes in the attitudes Americans expressed concerning piano lessons. Suddenly, taking piano lessons was not just meant for little girls. For many years it had been accepted as a fact that all great pianists were men. It was commonly felt that "Women lacked the physical, as well as the mental stamina to become a really fine artist." In spite of the fallacy of such idiotic statements, that concept was very prevalent among a vast number of people in America prior to Van Cliburn's journey to Russia. Yet, often these same people who felt only men had the power and strength to become fine pianists also felt that taking piano lessons was only for "sissies."

Well, after Van Cliburn "showed them Russians" a thing or two, little boys were suddenly being encouraged, if not forcefully persuaded, to take piano lessons. Every Tom, Dick, Michael and Harold, whose family could afford a piano, began taking lessons. With such a plethora of students one would think that a great advancement would have been made toward the appreciation of fine music. Unfortunately, the majority of those students became drop-outs long before they had a chance to become good pianists, or even to begin to appreciate fine music.

One could probably find numerous reasons for the number of children who began piano lessons and then stopped; but, incompetence was, more than likely, the primary culprit. At the time, parents and students had no real understanding of the enormous amount of study, concentration and physical stamina that it takes to become a fine pianist. Many parents had been duped into believing that one could learn to play the piano in ten easy lessons, as promised by so many magazine ads. Even more devastating was the fact that so many parents felt that the very best teacher, or the very best instrument, was not necessary for the beginner. Just any teacher or just any beat-up old piano was all that was needed to start. If their child showed progress and enjoyed taking lessons, a better teacher (usually meaning a more expensive one) could come later, along with a better instrument.

Just how, in the name of heaven, these parents ever came to the conclusion that a child could learn to play the piano by taking lessons from an incompetent teacher, or that their child could develop an ear for good music by practicing on a piano which had long lost its usefulness, is beyond my imagination. While it is true that a few students made progress in spite of the condition of the piano, provided that they had a good teacher, the majority of these students simply dropped out.

44

DON'T PUT THE TEACHER DOWN FOR TRAVELING

I have just finished reading a chapter from a book in which the author expounds her theories as to what one should do when searching for a piano teacher. Although this author presents some sound advice, I found several of her statements highly objectionable. I was appalled at one statement in which she states: "Parents should not even consider engaging a teacher who will consent to come to their home to teach their child. No reputable teacher has the time to travel to a student's home to teach."

When I recited this statement to several of my colleagues, I was even more shocked to find that so many of these teachers were in agreement with the author. It is sad that so many teachers have been misguided into believing that teachers who travel to homes to teach are less qualified to teach than teachers who teach in a studio. I fear that this attitude has descended from teachers who were imbued with more than their share of unadulterated snobbery. While I certainly, in no way, would consider the teachers with whom I discussed this attitude as possessing even the slightest trace of snobbery, they seemed unaware that the statement has no basis in truth.

Although, I would certainly agree that a studio, in most cases, presents an atmosphere that is more conducive to teaching, it is ludicrous to believe that the qualification of teachers is impeded by their willingness to go to homes.

Today, many well-qualified teachers are forced to pursue this course. For an ever-increasing number of teachers, the high cost of maintaining a studio is making it impossible for them to teach without going to homes. Often, teachers find it necessary to live in multiple dwellings where they are lucky if the landlord will allow them to practice. A steady stream of students, coming and going, would be completely out of the question. Teachers who have the audacity to question the qualifications of a teacher merely on the grounds that this teacher agrees to go to the home of a student to teach might consider this little anecdote which was related to me several years ago:

"Once there was this little girl who wanted to have piano lessons; but, her parents refused to let her out of the house and into the cold to get to a piano teacher. There was a reason for this, of course. That little girl had nearly died from an infection of the throat since she was allergic to the cold. As luck would have it, the parents found a young man who would come to their house to give this little girl lessons." The person who told me that story was none other than the renowned pianist and teacher, Rosina Lhevinne. Madam Lhevinne was the little girl in that story. The teacher who agreed to come to the home was Josef Lhevinne. I think that should put to rest any notion that teachers who go to homes to teach are in some way inferior to those who will only teach in their studio.

I have often told this story, but I believe it bears repeating.

45

A LICENSE DOES NOT A TEACHER MAKE

From time to time, some teachers and professors speak out in favor of licensing teachers in order to improve the teaching standards of private music teachers. These advocates of having music teachers licensed remind us that our public school teachers have, for many years, been required to be licensed.

Indeed they have. Yet, from all reports there has been little, if any, improvement in the education of our children due to this requirement. To the contrary, we have students entering the business world who are unable to compose a simple letter. Many are incapable of reading above a sixth grade level. Their spelling is a disgrace.

Of course, there are many fine teachers in our public school system and there are exceptional students. But can one really state, unequivocally, that the number of fine teachers that we find throughout the system is a result of licensing? I think not. There are no simplistic answers to the many questions that could be asked concerning what makes a good teacher. An exemplary education is no guarantee that such education will result in a fine teacher. It has been proven many times over that some of our most highly educated and masterful technicians are often lousy teachers.

Often, some of our finest musicians and concert artists are totally incpt when it comes to teaching. It takes more, much more, than an education to make a great teacher. Without a doubt, the ability to perform is a prerequisite for any teacher, but that ability alone is insufficient in the makings of an outstanding teacher.

Unfortunately, many of our educators in the field of music seem to feel that a degree in performance is a license to teach. All too often these individuals simply do not have an aptitude for teaching. One may have all the skills it takes for performing, but unless that individual has the ability to impart those skills upon the student, he or she will be a failure as a teacher.

Indeed, "A License Does Not A Teacher Make."

46

GOOD PERFORMERS ARE
CRAWLING OUT OF THE WALLS

Several years ago, upon my return to California, I applied for and was accepted as a member of the Music Teachers' Association of California. One could search far and wide and still not find a group of more dedicated teachers than the members of that Association. These teachers are constantly in search of ways to improve their teaching methods. Their Certificate of Merit Program is a splendid example of what Music Teachers can do to improve the musical education of our young students.

This program evaluates the progress a student makes, in performance and in theory, on a yearly basis. The evaluators are given special training and are sent to the various counties throughout the state to test each and every student on an individual basis. There is a well-planned syllabus that defines the specific requirements for each level (Preparatory through Level 10). There are Branch Honors Recitals and Yearly Convention Recitals students may take part in after they have successfully passed specified levels. This program not only promotes good teaching, it also assures the parents that their child is progressing.

One of the fine points of this yearly evaluation is that the adjudicators are never from the same county in which the various students are taught. In addition, in order to assure that a fair and unbiased evaluation is rendered, the teachers are simply listed by a code number. This procedure eliminates the possibility that an adjudicator might be inclined to show favoritism for the students of any particular teacher.

As an added benefit, the teachers, after having carefully given performance evaluations of their students, as well as the written theory tests, can readily ascertain their strong and weak points in teaching.

Since each student receives a private evaluation, the system is relatively non-competitive. As for the written theory exams the student receives either a passing grade or a recommendation that he or she needs more work. This allows the student to complete the recommended study and still enroll on a higher level should that student, upon the approval of their teacher, desire to do so.

Of course, one might argue that since those students who pass are given a Certificate of Merit, that that is a form of competition; however, since this is basically a matter which will only come up between the student, the parents and the teacher, the competitive aspect is kept to a minimum.

I think that this relatively non-competitive aspect of this program is admirable and I hope and trust this system will prevail in the future. Nothing could be any more detrimental to this program than for the MTAC to start giving out prizes, or cash awards, to students who get the highest marks in performance or in theory. The whole purpose of this program is to evaluate a student's progress on a yearly basis; it is not a program in which students should be encouraged to compete against other students.

There is no doubt that this program has resulted in an overwhelming number of very fine performers. As one of my colleagues so aptly stated: "Good performers are coming out of the walls."

The question, of course, remains, what in the world are we going to do with them?

47

DOWN MEMORY LANE

I fell in love with California in the summer of 1942, having spent that summer with an uncle who had a small farm in El Cajon, a short drive from San Diego. At that time, that part of California was indescribably beautiful. Atop any of the numerous hills surrounding El Cajon one could look over miles and miles of orange and lemon groves. There were also vast acreages covered with avocado and walnut trees. The center of downtown El Cajon consisted of a small general store (including a post-office, feed store, drug store and, I believe, the Greyhound Bus Depot). It was not a large store and I don't recall having seen any other stores around.

With the GI Bill at my disposal, I decided to attend the Los Angeles Conservatory of Music and Arts. In addition to the theory and academic courses required, I was assigned to study the piano with Catherine Coleman. After several months with Miss Coleman, she advised me that Madam Lhevinne was coming out from New York to give a six weeks master class. It was Miss Coleman's desire that I audition for this class in order to study privately with Madam Lhevinne while she was in California. I was not enthusiastic. First of all, I had never heard of Madam Lhevinne. Secondly, I was not desirous of becoming a concert pianist. My primary interest was to be a good teacher. I had wanted to be a piano teacher as far back as I could remember. But upon Miss Coleman's insistence, I agreed to audition.

Well, let me tell you, I was overwhelmed with that lady with the thick Russian accent from the first time I saw her. Those deep dark brown eyes of hers seemed to penetrate one's soul; but it was an affectionate and loving penetration. She was a paradox. Her regal bearing kept one at a distance; yet she was that loving grandmother upon whose lap one wanted to jump and give her a big hug. For me, it was love at first sight.

After several weeks of study with Madam Lhevinne, she came into the room in which I was practicing and asked me to join her for lunch. She wanted to go to the park, get some "hotdogs" and soft drinks, rent a paddle boat and have lunch on the lake in Westlake Park.

In the middle of the lake, as we sat eating and drinking, she said that what she really wanted to do was to talk about my future.

"I think it is very admirable that you want to teach," she said. "Students who usually come to me all want to play for a living. Only a very few will ever reach that goal. Many will end up teaching and their hearts will not be in it. I don't think they will make good teachers. Most will simply give up music and go into other fields. Teaching is an honorable profession. A good teacher must not only be an exceptional pianist, he must have more than the ability to play. A good teacher must go beyond just being a fine pianist."

After that little speech, Madam Lhevinne asked me many personal questions: "Did I have a piano where I was staying for practice? Could I live on the allowance from the GI Bill? How much money did I make on my part-time job? How much did I need for food and clothing?"

I was taken aback by all those personal questions but I answered them as honestly as I could. Not once did Madam Lhevinne even hint as to the reason for this interrogation. I found out two days later when the dean of the school called me into her office and asked if I would consider becoming a member of the faculty with the understanding that I was to give up my part-time job and devote full-time to practicing, studying and teaching. She said that Madam Lhevinne and she had gone over my financial requirements and that I would be given enough students to cover those requirements.

Needless to say, I accepted.

48

MUSIC AS AN ADVOCATION

I was asking the question about what we are going to do with all of the piano students we piano teachers are turning out and I got side-tracked down memory lane. We older passengers on this planet are prone to do that from time to time.

Sure, good performers are coming out of the walls. Why not? The more, the merrier. As I have often stated, there is probably no better way to spend one's time than making music. Certainly it is one of the most pleasurable pursuits conceivable.

The problem is not that there are so many good performers; the problem is that so many of us who teach these students prime them for a career in music. We present them in recitals. We place them in competitions. We make a nervous wreck out of a good many of them and when they go off to college they rarely touch the piano again, providing, of course, that they haven't dropped-out long before they get to college.

Now I'm not advocating that students should not be given the very best training a teacher can give. No student will ever be able to enjoy playing the piano if he or she does not have a very thorough musical education. No students will ever be able to fully enjoy playing the piano unless they have been thoroughly grounded with the basics. Students should not be deceived into believing that learning to play the piano is all "fun and games." It is not. It requires a lot of work to learn to play the piano well. A lot of study. Many hours of diligent practice. But the final goal should be that these students will have the ability to sit down and make music for the sake of making music.

Of course, we should have musical festivals in which students should be able to participate. Participate, not compete! We should encourage our students to play for each other, to join others in duets and to perform chamber music. We should encourage parents to invite other students into their homes for "musicales." We should have recitals for students who wish to perform in them and outlaw that idiotic rule that a student cannot play in a recital unless the compositions are memorized. If students want to use their music they should be encouraged to do so; the purpose of a recital should be to present good music, not to display memory freaks.*

Of course, every student should be taught to strive for perfection. There is no greater reward to be had than the knowledge that we have performed a composition to our own satisfaction.

---

* A few days after I had written that the purpose of a recital should be to present good music, not to display memory freaks, it dawned upon me that I was again quoting Madam Lhevinne, or at least paraphrasing her statement.

In a master class back in the late forties, she had reminded us that when she was studying at the Moscow Conservatory very little stress had been placed on the importance of memorizing compositions. Students were always allowed to use the music when performing. She said that much more importance was placed on musicianship. She went on to say that she once had to give a performance of a concerto in New York and had gotten "cold feet" because she had, only a few days prior, heard Myra Hess give a performance in which she used the music. Madam Lhevinne said that she was in a quandary for days, trying to decide whether or not she too should use music.

Then she added, "I sometimes wonder if we are not trying to produce memory freaks instead of fine musicians. Sometimes I think students are much more concerned with a slip of the memory than they are about the quality of music they make."

49

MARIAN ANDERSON

Before I got on that tangent about what we should do with our students, I had given vent to nostalgic memories concerning my early years at the Los Angeles Conservatory of Music and Arts. Well, a recent review of a book by Rosalyn M. Story, "And So I Sing," triggered other memories of the past. The book is about African-American Divas of Opera and Concerts with an account of Marian Anderson and her episode with the Daughters of the American Revolution being the centerpiece of the book.

My first encounter with the artistry of Marian Anderson was by way of recordings. It was a time when high schools throughout the country still considered music important enough to provide a course in music appreciation for students who chose to take such a course. The instructor of this class was ecstatic in his appraisal of this young "Negro" singer. The term "Black" was not then in common usage. After having listened to the recordings of this great star, I don't believe there could have been found one student amongst the entire class that had not fallen in love with Miss Anderson. Ironically, the school which had presented that class was none other than "Little Rock Senior High School," later changed to "Central High"—the same school which, with the backing of the Governor of Arkansas, had refused to integrate until they were forced to do so by the use of federal troops.

Needless to say, after having read the review, I rushed out and bought the book.

50

GOSPEL ACCORDING TO SAINT FUNDAMENTALIS

While reading "And So I Sing," it became apparent that the "Blacks" have come a long way since the days when the Daughters of the American Revolution refused to grant permission for Marian Anderson to sing at Constitutional Hall in Washington, D.C.; but, unfortunately, racism is still with us. A few summers ago, as an example, I was traveling by bus from New York to San Francisco, when the bus passed through the Bible Belt. The bus stopped to pick up a passenger at some small town along the way. A white passenger got on the bus, paid her fare to the next small town but remained standing.

"Take a seat, lady," the bus driver commanded. There was only one seat on the bus and that happened to be beside a "Black" passenger. The newly arrive passenger remained standing.

"Either you take a seat, lady," the driver repeated, "Or, we'll have to just sit here."

She mumbled that she was not going to sit down beside "no nigra."

A young white man got up and gave her his seat and then sat down beside the "Black."

As the newly arrived passenger sat down she remarked, "Thank you, son. The Good Lord always provides a way."

Upon remembering that incident, I sat down and wrote:

So, that's it. The Lord will provide a way. All one has to do is follow the Gospel According to Saint Fundamentalis:

Money is my shepherd; with it I shall not want. It maketh me to bed down in luxury. With enough of it I can surely be comforted for the rest of my days.

Remember thou the Golden Rule: Do others before they do thee.

"Vengeance is yours," sayeth the Lord. "Avenge thine enemies and make life a living hell for those who do not agree with thee."

When Saint Peter took up his sword and cut off the ear of the soldier, the Lord said, "Bravo, Peter! It is good you taketh up the sword; for, it is written that those who live by the sword shall have peace."

Love God above all things and maketh certain thou screweth thy neighbor before he screweth thee.

The Lord sayeth: "It has been written, an eye for an eye and a tooth for a tooth, but, I say to thee, 'if thou be struck on one cheek, striketh thee back with enough force that he that striketh thee will thinketh thrice before he striketh thee twice.'"

Giveth not unless thou first receiveth; for, the Lord sayeth, "It is better to receive than to give."

And, giveth not to those in need, lest thou encourage them to be shiftless.

Feed the wealthy; let the poor take care of the poor; for, it is written that thou are not thy brother's keeper.

Remember the Beatitude; "Blessed are the rich; for, they shall have plenty."

If thou be not rich, remember to give to the landlord what is due and the rest to the collection plate, lest those who bringeth you these words be not comforted.

Love thy neighbor, unless he be a Jew, a Catholic, an Indian, a Black, an Asian, an Hispanic, a Homosexual, a Democrat, or anyone who is not a pure-bred white Born Again Christian like thee; for the Lord has not commanded thee to love thine enemies.

If a man stealeth thy coat and thou findeth him, taketh back not just thy coat, taketh also his shirt and trousers so that he shall not stealteth from thee again.

If thou be rich and findeth a way to taketh that which does not belong to thee, feel not guilty when thou taketh it; for, since it is written that the Lord giveth and the Lord taketh, what righteous man would dare to question the wisdom of the Lord for having given it to thee.

If thou have plenty for the rest of thy days, find thee ways to get more; for, the rich man will surely ride his camel through the gates of heaven as easily as threading the eye of a needle.

It is written: "What does it profit a man if he gains his soul and loses the whole world."

If thou have sinned maketh certain thou cast the first stone, lest the accused point a finger at thee.

When thou pray, pray in public; for, it is written: "When thou pray, come out of thy closet and shout thy prayers from the rooftops." Closets are reserved for queens.

If thou be not caught in sin, be mindful that it is better to make war than to make love.

Remember to condemn thy fellow man; for, it is written: "Judge a lot; lest thou be judged."

PETER FUNDAMENTALIS
Bible Belt, U.S.A. Circa 1990

51

THE LAND OF OPPORTUNITY

You know, there's been a lot of apathy on the part of the general public when it comes to politics. Yet, there is no doubt that politicians can bring about many changes. President Reagan, for example, made it much easier for the very wealthy to increase their wealth, at the expense of the lower and upper-middle class. One of the finest report cards on what the Republicans and Democrats have done for the country has been supplied for us by Kevin Phillips in his book entitled: "The Politics of Rich and Poor." This should be required reading for anyone interested in what is happening to this country.

No doubt, politicians can bring about many changes, for the better or worse. As a teacher for a good part of my life, it is only natural that I am concerned with what these politicians do in the way of improving the education of our young generation. Of course, there has been great strides made in the past few decades; but, it is obvious from all reports that there is much more to do, particularly in the field of the arts. I often wonder what has happened in our more rural sections. Hopefully, there has been some improvements made since the late forties and early fifties.

When I left Los Angeles, in the late forties, and returned to Arkansas, for example, there was little opportunity for a good education for a sizable portion of young students in that "Land of Opportunity" when it came to the arts. Schools in general were underfunded and, as is nearly always the case, the arts were considered non-essentials. This, in spite of the fact that history shows that civilizations and nations have progressed in direct proportion to the stress that has been placed on the importance of the arts, remains a blight on our educational system.

The motto of the state of Arkansas, "The Land of Opportunity," certainly did not apply to musicians at the time of my return. Although parents and students seemed to hunger for the arts, there simply were no funds available for these courses.

My first job consisted of teaching piano to about thirty young children in a small rural school just south of Little Rock. The school supplied the piano. The students paid a nominal fee for the lessons. Unfortunately, it was a complete fiasco, even though I remained for the school year. First of all, the piano was located in the auditorium and the centrally located wood-burning, pot-bellied stove simply was not capable of supplying the heat needed for the area. The children came to their lessons in overcoats and heavy wool gloves. Since I sat there dressed in the same attire, I did not have the heart to ask the children to remove their gloves; but it would have been impossible without them. Very little progress was made; however, when any child learned to play a simple tune, gratification was amply shown. I'll never forget the pride revealed in the face of one little girl who had learned to play a little tune based upon a theme from La Boheme.

Mimi's tiny frozen hands could not have been any colder than the hands of that little girl who sat down to play the piano in the auditorium of that small country school on that cold, cold, day in rural Arkansas.

Postscript:

Once again I have turned back the pages of these memories to express the fact that it is now my understanding that many changes for the better, educationally, have taken place as a result of the splendid efforts put forth by Hillary and Bill Clinton, when Bill Clinton was the Governor of Arkansas.

52

MIMI COMES TO NEW GUINEA

My first encounter with "Thy Tiny Hands Are Frozen," came about in the steamy jungles of New Guinea. A soldier, whose name I remember as being Leonard, approached me one day in the mess hall and informed me that he had heard that I was a pianist. He asked me if I would accompany him at the base recreation center. I agreed. I'm afraid that I was not a good sight reader but Leonard made a big hit with his high "C." Leonard had a magnificent voice and we continued to get together at the recreation center as long as I remained in New Guinea.

Leonard also introduced me to the Master Sergeant from the base headquarters who was also very much interested in music. Somehow, this sergeant had been able to obtain a large collection of classical records and he gave weekly recorded recitals at the base recreation center. It was well attended, particularly by the Australians who happened to be at the same base.

I lost contact with Leonard after I left New Guinea; he remained in New Guinea and I went on to the Philippines and eventually to Japan.

After the war, while I was attending the Los Angeles conservatory of Music and Arts, I was pleasantly surprised to find that Leonard was also studying voice there; but I again lost contact with him after I left Los Angeles to go to New York to study with Madam Lhevinne. Actually, although it was my intention to go directly to New York, I went home to Little Rock on the way for a short visit and that visit lasted almost a year. During that year, I taught a course in music appreciation in a parochial school in Little Rock, had a class of very fine students at a high school in England, Arkansas, as well as the students I mentioned in my previous comments about "The Land of Opportunity."

I often wonder what ever happened to Leonard.

The only other musician I remember having contact with while I was in the Army, was a pianist I met while I was in an army field hospital in the Philippines. On several occasions, I sat quietly in back of the recreation hall listening to him practice Rachmaninov's Piano Concerto Number Two. I refrained from remaining long enough for any introductions, primarily out of concern that I didn't want to come close enough for him to catch the rather severe case of conjunctivitis for which I was being treated.

Years later, however, I saw him walking down the hall at Juilliard. I was in a rush to get to a Master Class of Madam Lhevinne's; so, once again, I failed to introduce myself and I don't believe he remembered me from the Philippines.

53

HELEN SCOVILLE

As we mortals travel through life, we become friendly with many people; but few become friends. What is sad, however, is the fact that we so often neglect those whom we know to be our true friends.

For years I studied piano with Helen Scoville at the Manhattan School of Music. For several years, Helen had been an assistant to the late Ernest Hutchison when he was teaching at The Juilliard School of Music in New York. Before that, she had toured the United States and Europe as a concert pianist, receiving rave reviews in every city in which she played.

Helen was also an extremely gifted teacher. After I left the Manhattan School of Music, I used to go down to her apartment in the Village where we would spend hours discussing music, philosophy, art and anything else that happened to be on our minds.

Although Helen was an exceptionally warm person, she rarely complimented her students. When she did praise your work, however, she had the ability to, with few words, make you feel as though you were walking on cloud nine. She would, for example, simply state: "You played that like a real pro." But such statements didn't come often; when they did, usually after many months of hard work, you knew that it was an honest evaluation.

When Helen retired she moved to Switzerland. For several years we corresponded. As is often the case, however, our letters to and from each other grew further apart. It was only after I moved back to California that I learned from a former student that she had returned to New York and had died there about a year later.

I suppose everyone has had similar experiences. It is sad, though. I guess we could all kick ourselves in the rear when we allow friends to drift away without keeping in contact with them.

Helen and I often discussed the philosophy of reincarnation. Although she had several reservations about reincarnation, she was not adamantly opposed to the idea. She was convinced that people like Mozart could not have been born with the musical knowledge he displayed at such an early age without having lived before. "Sometimes, I am convinced," she said, "that it takes more than one life-time to become a great musician."

But Helen often expressed her belief that the only reason that we are put on this earth is to learn how to become an understanding, loving and compassionate human being. If that is the case, I may be in for a disappointment in my hope that Helen and I will meet again the next time around. I believe there is a strong possibility that Helen had reached that state of perfection wherein she will not have to return. For me, well, I'm afraid I have a lot to learn.

Note:

Those who had the fortune to know Helen Scoville will, no doubt, find the following information interesting and those who did not know her will find it informative.

From a copy of a publicity brochure found among some of my memorabilia:

Helen Scoville, brilliant young American pianist, has been heard in recital and with orchestra in the United States, Canada, Sweden, Norway, Denmark, Germany and Holland.

Miss Scoville studied with Ernest Hutcheson and is a graduate of The Juillard School of Music. Her New York debut was a triumphant success, and she was immediately recognized as an artist of unusual musical skill.

And, for the reviews:

Has command of a fleet and thundering technique, and plays with the temperament of a virtuoso.
New York Times

Displayed command of style and interpretation—attractive and varied quality of tone—encompassed rapid and brilliant passages with skill and accuracy. A pianist of unusual interest.
New York Journal-American

Brilliant technique and a wide range of tone color, with a vigorous forceful style and command of spectacular effects—flair for the dramatic—velvety tone and poetic insight—keen sense of rhythm.
The Glove & Mail, Toronto

The hands to play and the brains to direct them—imagination and brilliant technique.
Chicago Daily Tribune

An excellent pianist, a real virtuoso with masculine* power and a very refined touch.
Hationen, Oslo

*There is that underhanded remark concerning the difference between a man's performance and a woman's performance, no doubt implying that powerful playing was not the norm for a woman.

Unusual power of formation, technical skill, but employed as a means and under clever control.
> Svenska Tagbladet, Stockholm

This artist has a great pictorial faculty and a vivid imagination.
> Scoialdem, Copenhagen

Broad and impetuous mastery of the keyboard—full and luscious tone—proportion, movement, power.
> Chicago Evening Journal

Brilliant and highly flavored reading—triumphed all along the line—her next visit will need no herald save her own reputation.
> Chicago Evening American

A gift for interpretation—a pianist whose playing delighted.
> Chicago Daily News

Fabulously clever fingers led by finest thoughts—her artistic interpretation was impressive and significant.
> Deutsche Allegemeine Zeitung, Berlin

Her interpretations are captivating and full of temperament.
> Germania, Berlin

A technically significant, fine, sensitive and profoundly musical pianist.
> Neueste Nachrichten, Leipzig

54

POZANSKY AND TCHAIKOVSKY

A while back, I mentioned that very little is known about the private life of Peter Tchaikovsky. Now, we can put that assertion to rest. Alexander Poznansky, a graduate from the University of Leningrad, has, after more than a decade of painstaking research, given us a book of facts, rather than fancies, about the life of this composer. Without a doubt, this is probably the fullest and most revealing account ever to be written concerning the private life of Tchaikovsky.

By way of letters, diaries and memoirs, Mr. Poxnansky has brought to life a vast amount of factual material, much of which has been ignored by other biographers. No doubt, much of the previously neglected material was due to the extreme censorship imposed by the Russian government.

We learn, for example, that the boarding schools in Russia, as well as those throughout Europe and England, were rampant with sexual activity, particularly between boys who came from families of upper and lower gentry. These activities, for the most part, were looked upon as being normal behavior and were, more or less, openly tolerated as long as no public scandal resulted, bringing to mind the often stated remark attributed to Queen Victoria: "I don't care what they do, as long as they don't do it in the streets and scare the horses."

In this monumental biography, "Tchaikovsky, The Quest for the Inner Man," Alexander Poznansky traces the inner life of Tchaikovsky through the pre-revolutionary Russian culture in which he lived, as well as revealing, perhaps for the first time, Tchaikovsky's relationship with the European homosexual underground.

This, however, is not one of those sensational biographies that one might expect from scandal prone authors. In the words of one reviewer from one of our most prestigious universities: "This book is written not only with seldom equalled erudition but also with compassion an sympathy. For the first time ever we meet Tchaikovsky as he was and read about his life as he lived it."

Certainly no finer account of the life of Tchaikovsky is likely to be found and it is just as likely that a more thorough account of this composer's life will never be forthcoming.

55

DEAR DR. FREUD

Sometimes I think we piano teachers are expected to be substitute parents, parish priest and Dr. Freud, all rolled into one package. If you're not a good sounding board, I doubt very seriously that you will ever make a good piano teacher. I don't advocate that teachers should, during the course of a piano lesson, dispense with advice which should rightly come from professionals who have the expertise to deal with students who need professional help. But students are often simply in need of a shoulder to lean on, figuratively speaking, of course.

Just recently, for example, I had a sixteen-year-old boy who could not concentrate on his lesson. Suddenly he stopped playing and asked me, "Mr. Barnhart, what do you think of the 'Gulf War?'"

"I think it stinks," I replied. "Why do you ask?"

Well, he just talked on and on. I didn't interrupt him. It was obvious that he was afraid that he would eventually be called upon to serve in that war.

Of course, I could have interrupted him and told him that we better get back to the piano lesson; but I felt it was much more important to just let him talk. I couldn't offer him any words of comfort. As a matter of fact, I hardly spoke at all except to agree with him when he said he thought that President Bush should have negotiated a settlement rather than sending in troops to the Gulf War.

Just before his time was up, he said, "Well, I guess if I have to go, I'll have to go; but maybe it will be over by the time I'm old enough to go."

When I related this incident to one of my colleagues she advised me, rather smugly, I think, that it was our duty to teach piano, not to carry on a lengthy conversation that didn't pertain to the piano lesson. "The parents are paying us to teach piano," she added.

I didn't respond; but the truth is I was thinking, "How callous can one get?" But that was an unfair thought. In truth, that teacher is a fine teacher and furthermore, I know for a fact that she does, from time to time, use lesson time to discuss problems with her students which have nothing to do with the study of piano.

What do you say to a small child who is bursting with excitement about some event that is going to take place after the lesson? Do you spend ten minutes of lesson time trying to get her to settle down or, perhaps, five minutes for her to tell you about it, knowing that she will then settle down?

56

DEATH OF A SPOKESMAN

Immediately following the death of Lenny Bernstein, most of the papers throughout the country carried articles concerning his life and career. One columnist mentioned that he had left the Boston Bay Area early in his career to take residence in New York. This columnist claimed that he did so because his controversial life-style would have been detrimental to him amongst staid Bostonians and the fact that his being a Jew would be an asset in New York.

It is hard for me to believe that Boston, being one of the most sophisticated cities on the East Coast, would have held Lenny back because of his Jewishness; but, to be sure, back in the thirties and forties, there certainly was an enormous amount of anti-Semitism throughout the country. The year I spent teaching in and around Little Rock, for example, I had been confronted by the mother of one of my students, after having announced that I would be leaving to go to New York. This mother was very distraught. She simply didn't know where she was going to find another teacher. Many of the fine piano teachers were not accepting any new students. I explained to her that I had spoken with one of the best teachers in Little Rock and that I was fairly certain that he would accept her son.

"I couldn't send Paul to him," this mother replied.

"Unless you know something that I don't, this teacher has a

reputation for being one of the finest teachers in Little Rock," I stressed.

"I know that," she said, "but he's Jewish. Children are influenced by their teachers. They see them as a role model."

"I see," I replied. "I suppose that does make a difference. But, tell me, did you know that I was a Jew?"

Her jaw dropped at least an inch and a half. She sat down. I thought she was going to faint. "No, I didn't know that. If I had known, I would have never let Paul study with you. I'm afraid that I will have to give this some thought."

Indeed, she must have given it a lot of thought. A couple of weeks later, I received a note of apology, as well as word informing me that the teacher I had recommended had accepted her son as a student.

Perhaps I should not have said that I was Jewish; but it did me good to see her squirm. I was lucky that she did not question me about Judaism. Of course, had I told her that I was Catholic, she would have been just as upset. In the land of southern WASPS in the forties, where Klansmen were heroes, it made little difference whether you were a foreigner, a Catholic, a Jew or a Negro.

But getting back to Mr. Bernstein, I'm certain he will be remembered as one of music's greatest spokesman. I have mentioned his name on previous occasions; but, his death is a great loss to the world of music. He probably did more to bring about the appreciation of serious music in America than any other person in the entire country. As a conductor, he brought an emotional penetration, as well as vigor, to millions from coast to coast. His "Young Person's Concerts" in the 1960's proved that he had a rare gift as a communicator as well as an educator. He brought about a general understanding of classical music to many who would never have otherwise been exposed to this music.

He shall be missed; but, for the sake of music, we must have hope that another bright star will come along soon to take over where he left off. In the meantime, we must be content in knowing that the music world is much better for having had him as its spokesman for all these years.

57

ANOTHER TRAGIC LOSS

A friend, at the Baldwin's Piano Store here in the Bay Area, has just informed me that one of their shining stars has flickered out. I was quite taken aback by this sad news, as well as surprised that I had not read about the death of Jorge Bolet in the papers. Evidently his passing had happened around the same time that Leonard Bernstein had died. I suppose not too much was written up about Bolet here in the Bay Area's local papers.

In spite of the fact that Bolet was hailed as "One of the great Liszt pianists of the century" by several critics, including Harold Schonberg of the New York Times, this recognition did not come over night. If my memory serves me correctly, there was a great deal of talk about this outstanding performer from Cuba back in the early fifties. Everyone who had heard him felt that he should have been given much more publicity than was afforded him at the time. All too well do I remember my first attendance at one of his concerts. As a matter of fact, it was my friend Tom who had insisted that I accompany him to the Lower East Side to hear this young marvel. The auditorium was rather shabby but the audience consisted of students and other piano enthusiasts from all over Manhattan who were more than anxious to hear this remarkable pianist. His performance that evening gave ample proof that a musical giant was in the making.

Well, although those who heard Mr. Bolet during that period of time felt that he was ready to confront the world, this confrontation did not take place. For several years it seemed as though Bolet would simply join that multitude of pianists who never made it to the top.

But recognition did finally come. For a good many it seemed that this giant of a man, as well as a giant at the keyboard, had suddenly sprung out of nowhere. To those who knew better, it was obvious that Mr. Bolet had struggled very hard to get the recognition that he deserved.

Indeed, Bolet's talent was rare; but, more important was the fact that he had had the tenacity and total dedication that his art required. Without this commitment, no artist can ever hope to reach the top.

58

"LISTENING" MAKES THE DIFFERENCE

As a teacher, I am often asked what makes one student of the piano stand out from others. Is there any one thing that a student can do to improve upon his or her playing?

The answer to that question was often supplied to me by Madam Lhevinne: "Listen!" I couldn't begin to count the number of times she impressed upon me the importance of listening. She often said, "The first thing, and perhaps the most important, for any student to do is to learn to listen. Many play; few listen. Listening well is an exercise of attention. True listening requires a tremendous amount of effort and total concentration. It is not an easy task. Young students do not learn this lesson easily; but, it should be one of the first priorities for a teacher to stress."

It would be absurd, of course, to expect a seven or eight year old to spend more than a few minutes each day at this task. However, if periods of prolonged listening are ever to be obtained, it is imperative that at least a small portion of each day's practice time be spent working toward that goal. Once a student has learned to apply total concentration to his or her practice time, a much greater rate of advancement will ensue.

In addition, of course, commitment is also very important. Without commitment, very little progress will ever be made. Total commitment may not guarantee success but it does more than any other factor to assure it.

59

MORE BOLET

No sooner had I finished writing the notes about Jorge Bolet, when I was sent an article from a New York paper, by my friend Tom; in this article, a critic had mentioned that Bolet had not received the recognition he had deserved until late in life. This critic said that in spite of the many accolades Mr. Bolet had received, including the Naumbergh Award in 1937, he had scarcely any engagements in the 40's and 50's.

The critic attributed this lack of recognition to the fact that Mr. Bolet played mostly Romantic Literature. Liszt, especially, was not "in" at the time. While it is true that many students, as well as teachers, back in the late 40's and early 50's frowned upon "show-off" pieces and Liszt's compositions, for the most part, certainly fit that category. I did not agree with this critic's assessment of Romantic Music in general. There were any number of pianists who were performing Schubert, Chopin, Schumann, Brahms and music from the so-called Romantic composers, including Franz Liszt and these performers were receiving ample attention. I felt, and still feel, that Mr. Bolet simply did not have the needed chutzpah to impress those people.

Again, that reminds me of a statement of Madam Lhevinne: "There is no doubt that one must have the good fortune to know people who have the right contacts to promote one's career. If, however, one is not fully prepared, all the luck in the world, and no matter what contacts one has, it will not help. One must be fully prepared and one must be exceptional. There is no room for mediocrity. Pianists must dedicate their lives to music."

Since everyone now knows that Mr. Bolet did not lack preparation, I think that it might be conceded that he was, perhaps through a personal shyness, unable to successfully enlist the help of those who could have pushed him into the limelight much sooner.

Whatever the reason, it is a shame that the world was, for many years, deprived of this wonderful pianist's supreme rendition of the Romantic Literature.

60

PREPARATION

Yes, Jorge Bolet was prepared; but how many students are prepared? Before that question can be answered, it seems to me that another question of the utmost importance should be answered first: Prepared for what? Not all students who study the piano do so with a musical career in mind; nor, should they. The majority of students study music for their own pleasure. Unfortunately, it takes several years of serious study and practice before a person can sit down and enjoy playing the piano without the help of a trained guide. Basically, students should receive a solid foundation in technique. This includes, note-reading, rhythm, touch, phrasing, as well as technical drills. This should also include exposure to vast amounts of piano literature available on each level in which the student is capable of playing.

It has been my experience to have noted that we piano teachers are all too often more concerned with grooming a student to perform a piece for a recital rather than teaching that student how to study and progress on his or her own time, with or without a teacher. I couldn't begin to count the many, many students who have come to me, after years of study, and have absolutely no experience of working on their own. When I assign a piece of music for them to learn, they will say: "Can you play it for me so I know what it sounds like?" They are completely dumbstruck when I respond: "You learn it first and then I'll play it for you."

They have no idea as to how to sit down and begin to work on a piece without having first heard it, so that they can begin to imitate. "Monkey see, monkey do!"

In addition to treating our students as if they were "young seals" to be trained by example and repetition, we often tend to concentrate on material that will bring attention to our students at recitals and competitions, paying little attention to material a student might need in order to become an independent student.

Of course, there is no harm done in "showing off" young gifted students, providing that we do not neglect giving them ample material in order to progress on their own steam, so to speak. We should not forget that students who have a paucity of repertoire will have very little chance of ever learning to enjoy music for music's sake.

Inevitably, the question will be asked as to how we can get our students to learn so much piano literature without becoming a "jack of all trades and master of none." Obviously, we must have our students learn how to bring some compositions to performance levels. At the same time, they should be playing through numerous compositions on a level in which they can learn these pieces rapidly and with a great degree of proficiency; but, not necessarily up to performance level.

Students will be amazed at how much piano literature they can learn by being consistent in their practicing and with a determination to learn something new, no matter how small, each day. I have read that a very famous and world-renowned teacher once said that by memorizing only one measure each day, a student could memorize the first book of Bach's Well-Tempered-Clavichord in two years. If I weren't such a procrastinator, I could have long proved that statement to be correct, if, indeed, it is an accurate statement. Perhaps, I should get started.

61

COMPETITIONS AND HONESTY

At the risk of being accused of being redundant, a recent broadcast of the 1990 Tchaikovsky Competitions on public television stations compels me to once again comment on competitions.

From my previous comments, I am sure that one would conclude that I am not a great admirer of competitions, in spite of the fact that I was ecstatic as anyone could be over Van Cliburn's victory back in the late fifties. There are many things in life in which we may become enthralled; yet, feel that they are wrong.

The Tchaikovsky Competitions, I believe most pianists will agree, are the piano olympics. I had always believed that these competitions were above criticism. This 1990 Competition, however, caused me some concern. First of all, several of the contestants expressed their feelings that favoritism existed among the judges, as well as attempted bribery on the part of the contestants. One judge, for example, said that for one short coaching lesson, he had been handed an envelope containing ten one hundred-dollar bills. He stated that he had returned the envelope and the money to the contestant, but apparently that contestant was not disqualified. Another contestant had brought along a Steinway Grand, worth several thousand dollars, ostensibly for her own use, which was to be donated to the Moscow Conservatory after the competitions were over. Once again, there was no apparent attempt made to disqualify that particular contestant.

One of the judges, who expressed his objections to these attempts of bribery, as well as stating that he felt these contestants should have been disqualified, admitted that he also had been coaching one of the students prior to the competition. Still, he was not asked to refrain from judging that particular student.

Well, so much for honesty when it comes to competitions.

62

EDUCATION AND MUSIC

The press, from time to time, informs us that budget cutting will wreak havoc on our schools. Music and Arts courses are usually the first subjects to go when there is a tightening of the belt, confirming the appalling disregard our educators have for the importance of music and arts as a part of the curriculum.

Although there has not been enough research to verify the left-brain-right-brain theory, there is ample proof that the serious study of music and the serious practice of a musical instrument do increase a student's ability to concentrate. This ability to concentrate, in turn, greatly enhances the possibility that a student will do better in other subjects. The study of music and arts is essential to the completeness of an education. When these ingredients are not supplied to each and every student it is a great loss to any society. Perhaps, by allowing our educators to place such a low priority on music and arts, it brings the message to our children that these things are of no importance. Yet, time after time, surveys and studies prove the opposite.

The author of "Lives of the Cell," biologists Lewis Thomas, for example, did a survey of the subjects undergraduates took before applying to medical schools. Surprisingly enough, sixty-six percent of those who applied who were music majors were admitted; whereas, only forty-four percent who had majored in biochemistry were admitted.

In a now well-known U.S. government report, it was stated that "the educational foundation of our society is being eroded by a rising tide of mediocrity that threatens our very future as a nation." Still, after having carefully analyzed this report, a special task force of scholars set forth recommendations for the improvement of our education system without once mentioning the importance of music and arts.

When scholars, such as the ones mentioned above, failed to recognize the importance of music and arts as part of a curriculum to improve our young minds, one has to wonder if we will, indeed, ever be able to rise above that tide of mediocrity which threatens us all.

63

ANOTHER MASTER LAID TO REST

There was a time when a performance of a musical composition was often accompanied by a story, a vogue that is, thankfully, long past. Music is now enjoyed for the sheer pleasure it brings to each listener without those silly, and often trite, embellishments.

However, certain compositions have traditionally suggested imaginative settings. One of those compositions is the sonata, by Ludwig van Beethoven, known as "Les Adieux," or "Farewell Sonata." This sonata is, indeed, suggestive, as is often described, of the parting, the absence and, finally, the return. The three movements are actually designated, by the composer, as: Das Lebewohl (Farewell), Die Abwesenheit (Absence) and Das Wiedershen (Return).

What brought that composition to mind was the announcement by the press that Rudolf Serkin had died, at the age of 88, in Guildford, Vermont, on the 8th of May, 1991. My very first encounter with "Les Adieux" took place about forty years ago as it was being performed on the stage of Carnegie Hall by that great and venerable pianist. Serkin was a master at the keyboard. Not only had he conquered the keyboard, he was a communicator of extreme music depth.

From that evening at Carnegie Hall, to this present day, "les Adieux" has remained one of my favorites. As interpreted by

Serkin, this sonata came to life. The first movement brought to mind the often unspoken sorrow that one feels at the parting of a dear friend. In the second movement, one could not help but detect the sadness and the longing for that friend. And, at last, Serkin seemed to revel in the return. Once could sense the sheer exhilaration taking place as the two friends meet again, grasping in tender, but robust embraces and, yes, even jumping and dancing with joy.

64

THREE CHEERS FOR A NON-COMPETITIVE COMPETITION

Just when I thought I had said enough about competitions, someone comes along with an idea that bears repeating. An article in the Piano Quarterly, written by Mark Wait, a professor of music at the College of Music, University of Colorado at Boulder, informs us of a new approach for giving support to young outstanding musicians in a non-competitive fashion.

This support comes by way of the Gilmore Artist and the Gilmore Young Artists Awards to be presented at the Irving S. Gilmore International Keyboard Festival to be held in Kalamazoo, Michigan. David Pocock, director of the festival, who worked for the Irving S. Gilmore Foundation, has a committee that goes around gathering taped performances of outstanding young students, without anyone knowing that they have been taped. These tapes are then handed to a group of world-renowned artists to select the student who will be nominated for the awards. After the nominations are made, an additional committee will travel incognito to hear these students perform in already scheduled live performances. No performer will ever know that he or she has been judged unless he or she actually has been notified that he or she is a winner.

The process for selecting the winners of this award is certainly an original approach to competitions. Since the nominees will not be subjected to the stigma of losing, this method for granting awards deserves watching closely and, perhaps, even imitating.

I say, "Three Cheers for this Non-Competitive Competition."

P.S. The May, 1991 edition of Clavier magazine reports that David Owen Norris, an English pianist, was selected as the winner of this non-competitive award and will receive approximately $250,000 in financial assistance, via cash awards as well as concert engagements within the next few years.

65

ONE DIRTY OLD MAN AT THE OPERA

A short time ago, I mentioned the fact that we have finally learned to appreciate music without having to embellish compositions with some trite story. Of course, as we all know, the reverse is not true. Stories are often enhanced by music. Opera is a prime example.

One of the most humorous reminders of this came to light several years when a student was playing Beethoven's "Variations on Nel Cor piu non mi sento" from the opera "La Molinari" by Giovanni Paisiello. The father of the young girl who was performing suddenly burst out laughing. My student, taken aback by this sudden display of uncontrolled emotion on the part of her father, stopped playing.

"I'm sorry," her father said. "Forgive me. Many years ago in the 'Old Country,' I attended a production of "La Molinari" and my daughter's playing reminded me of the Governor, who, in addition to sending a marriage proposal to Rachelina, was a dirty old man who chased the pretty girls, and even those that were not so pretty, around the stage in order to pinch their behinds. It's a very funny opera."

I have not been able to teach that composition since that day without remembering that student and her father.

66

PERFORMER ABUSE

Down through the years, students have often complained that they did not like to play for their parents or their parents' guests, because, in the words of the students: "They don't listen, anyway." How sad. Reminds me of the time I was invited to attend a pre-wedding dinner at the home of one of my former students in Hillsborough, that bastion of wealthy citizens just south of San Francisco, and the former residence of the late Bing Crosby, William Randolph Hearst and other well-known figures.

The parents of my former student were particularly anxious for me to attend, since they were having a pre-dinner concert to be performed by an émigré from the Soviet Union.

Indeed, the buffet dinner was beautifully and artistically displayed. The food, a gourmet's delight, would have satisfied the most discriminating palates. The caterer had done a splendid job of making the dinner an overwhelming success.

Unfortunately, no compliments are due the individual who was placed in charge of arranging and handling the pre-dinner concert. The supreme artistry of the pianist, a graduate of the Moscow Conservatory, was completely wasted on this screeching and bellowing crowd. One young basso, whose supercilious behavior was only overshadowed by his ability to pierce the atmosphere with a constant stream of noise, could easily have been mistaken for a foghorn. In addition, several guests, both male and female, who would have been at home at a hog-callers' convention, managed to stand directly behind the performer as they shouted and shrieked during the entire performance.

Since there had been no introduction of the artist before she sat down to play, it gradually became apparent that the majority of the guests had been unaware that the performer had been engaged to perform for them. Indeed, one "gentleman" complained that he had to raise his voice in order to be heard above "that woman who took over the piano." Unknowingly, he had voiced his complaint to the wife of the man who had actually been responsible for hiring the performer; yet, she made no attempt to subdue this man's attempt to out-vocalize the piano. To add insult to injury, another guest had the unmitigated gall to ask the performer if she would mind playing a little softer, since people were trying to talk.

Sadly, such mistreatment of performers is not rare. We have been so conditioned that we merely accept musicians as another commodity to be placed in the background, like music piped into an elevator or an office, but in a manner not to interrupt whatever else might be taking place.

Whenever an attempt to include a bit of culture at a social gathering is treated with such contempt, it reminds me of a statement attributed to Mahatma Gandhi:

"When asked what he thought about culture in America, Gandhi replied, "What a marvelous idea."

67

COMMON COURTESY

Indeed, the foregoing episode is sad; however, sometimes we find a parent who knows how to put a guest in his or her place when they lack the courtesy to remain quiet when a child has been asked to perform.

I'll never forget one New York mother who stopped her son from playing when one of her guests started talking and simply reminded that guest:

"You asked my son he should play the piano?

So, shut-up and listen, already!"

GOD, BLESS HER!

68

WHAT ABOUT THOSE PRODIGIES?

Most of us are thrilled when we are confronted with an extremely gifted child. But few of us take the time to consider the tremendously difficult task and responsibility the parents of a gifted child take upon themselves in order to develop a child's potential. First of all these parents must decide where the fine line must be drawn between a healthy and a non-healthy development.

In a book, written many years ago, "A Forbidden Childhood," the author describes almost unbelievable treatment of a young child prodigy by her father. We are told that this child was verbally and physically abused each time she struck a wrong note when practicing. Her father demanded absolute perfection. Although she became an outstanding pianist, it took many years in therapy, as an adult, to overcome the damage done to her as a young child.

Anton Rubenstein's mother, we are told, used to strap him to the piano bench and make him practice hour after hour as a young boy; yet, he became one of the world's greatest pianists, apparently without any damage to his mental state. And, we now know that Mozart was exploited by his father, although, from all accounts it seems as if young Mozart reveled in this exploitation.

Just recently, I attended a recital of a young girl, nine years old, who played a major program brilliantly and with insight and maturity far beyond her age. I learned that this child started playing the piano when she was three years of age. Presently, she routinely practices four hours each day. She is a straight "A" student in school and is, seemingly, a happy child, in spite of the fact that she has absolutely no social life.

Is it a healthy life? Who knows? Each child is different. Each set of parents is different. Who's to say what is healthy for any particular child?

Some parents are capable of handling prodigies; some are not.

69

TCHAIKOVSKY AND UNFOUNDED RUMORS

While browsing through a bookstore last Sunday, I came across Malcolm Forbes' "They Went That A-Way." Flipping through the pages, I came upon the subject of Pyotr Ilyich Tchaikovsky. Naturally, I had to take time to read what Mr. Forbes said about the death of Tchaikovsky.

In stating that Tchaikovsky died after drinking a contaminated glass of water, Mr. Forbes proceeded to repeat the old rumor that Tchaikovsky actually committed suicide after having gotten himself into a pickle when he wined and dined and you-know-what with some Russian aristocrat's nephew.

Alexander Poznansky, in his biography of Tchaikovsky—*The Quest for the Inner Man*, proves once and for all times that there is not even the slightest bit of evidence that that rumor is anything more than pure gossip, started by God only knows whom. Mr. Forbes says the story was presented by a Russian scholar in 1987 who got her story from an aged official at the Leningrad Museum. The names of neither the scholar nor the official were ever mentioned which leads one to doubt they even existed. At any rate, I got news for both of them: I heard the same rumor which supposedly came from a scholar who had access to the medical records of the doctor who treated Tchaikovsky. What's more, I heard that rumor back in the late forties when I was teaching at the Los Angeles Conservatory. No, I don't remember who told me; so don't ask. Let's face it, the story probably got started by gossip queen "Bossie." Or maybe the rumor got started by Oscar himself while residing at Reading Gaol.

No matter. People dote upon gossip, truthful or not. But the idea that Tchaikovsky committed suicide is as fallacious as the rumor, which was widely spread for generations, that the last two children of Clara Schumann had been fathered by Johannes Brahms.

70

A FEATHER IN OUR CAP

We piano teachers are often guilty of extolling the virtues of a musical education. Just as often, our educators seems to pay little heed to our praises and proclamations that learning to play an instrument greatly improves a child's ability to advance in other areas.

Occasionally someone comes along to whom we can look up to with pride and cite that individual as an example. What better example can we have than the country bumpkin from a small town in Arkansas. About the only fame for which the citizens of that scarcely populated village could, for many years, boast was the fact that they grew some of the largest watermelons in the world.

But along came a lad who moved from Hope to Hot Springs, mastered the saxophone, played in the high school band and won statewide competitions, was granted a Rhodes Scholarship, and received a law degree from Yale, and on the twentieth of January, nineteen-hundred and ninety-three, was sworn in as the 42nd President of the United States.

According to Stewart M. Powell, of the Washington Bureau of the San Francisco Examiner, President Clinton takes great pride in his self-discipline, a trait he attributes to his love for music. Mr. Powell quotes President Clinton as having once said:

"Music to me was kind of representative of everything I like most in life. It's beautiful and fun but very rigorous. If you wanted to be good, you had to work like crazy. It was a real relationship between effort and reward."

I think this admission from President Clinton is a "Feather in Our Cap" for all music teachers.

71

BUSH AND GRANT ON MUSIC

President Clinton's statement is quite a contrast to that of President Bush on the value of music. That contrast was expressed loud and clear at a special dinner held in San Antonio. Van Cliburn had supplied the entertainment for five Latin American presidents who had been brought together for a drug summit.

The next morning, over breakfast, President Bush remarked to the Mexican President, Carlos Salinas de Cortari:

"Well, I want to commend the Mexican delegation for staying awake through the piano music last night (Associated Press)."

It wasn't reported whether President Bush thought Van Cliburn's playing was at fault or whether he felt the music might be just a bit "high-brow" for the Mexican delegate. The Mexican president had the dignity not to comment. It was reported, however, that President Bush's national security advisor recoiled in mock surprise at the undiplomatic remark and exclaimed, "Mr. President!"

That statement by President Bush will probably go down in history as one of President Bush's most embarrassing diplomatic faux pas but I rather doubt that it will be quoted as often as has the quip that has been attributed to President U.S. Grant:

"I only know two tunes. One is 'Yankee Doodle Dandy;' the other one isn't."

72

MATCHMAKER

The video tape "In Celebration of the Piano," in which twenty-five Steinway Artists participated in a celebration of Steinway's 135th anniversary at Carnegie Hall, was actually held on June 2, 1988. Thanks to modern technology, however, we can enjoy watching, as well as hearing, these fine artists perform again and again.

Indeed, there are some remarkable performances on this tape. The ones that make the greatest impression upon me are:

Shura Cherkassky
Mr. Cherkassky performed the "March des Davidsbuendler" from the Carnival by Robert Schumann. His playing is powerful; yet, he plays with a rich, broad, warm and beautiful tone. He is truly one of the last of the romanticists from the Russian School of piano, born in Odessa in 1911.

Hai-Kyung Suli
Ms. Hai-Kyung, a pianist from Korea, performed "The Witches Dance" by Edward MacDowell. This pianist, although a fantastic technician, manages to maintain a marvelous singing tone throughout the entire performance of this technically demanding composition.

Cipa Dichter and Misha Dichter

The Dichters give a stunning performance of "Three Andalousian Dances" by Infante.

I was particularly delighted to hear Van Cliburn announce that the husband and wife team, Cipa and Misha Dichter, had met while studying in New York with Madam Lhevinne. I have no way of knowing whether or not Madam Lhevinne played any part in getting these two together; however, I would certainly not be surprised if she had. Madam Lhevinne had a reputation for assuming the role of a matchmaker." Hmmm?

73

BATTLES

Sometimes, it seems that teaching piano is nothing but one big battle. We battle with kids to practice. We battle with parents who refuse to set a schedule for practice time. We battle with kids who play too loud. We battle with kids who play too soft. We battle with kids to play the right notes. And, what a battle it is to get them to count.

Excuses? You bet! What do you say to a kid who says, "I couldn't practice (all week, mind you) because my mother made me take out the garbage?" Or, the kid who says he couldn't practice because his father was sick and stayed home from work on Tuesday? And what about the kid who went to visit his Grandma on Sunday?

But our battles are not always confined to parents and kids. Sometimes we teachers battle amongst ourselves. Which reminds me of a battle Madam Lhevinne often joked about. She said that many years ago, an article appeared in a magazine in which Mr. Hofmann, in an interview stated that he never practiced scales. According to Madam Lhevinne, Mr. Lhevinne was irate. He was afraid that young pianists would ask, "Why should I practice scales? If a great pianist like Mr. Hofmann doesn't practice scales, why should I?"

Josef Lhevinne, according to Madam Lhevinne, immediately sat down and wrote to the magazine, "How dare Mr. Hofmann give young students the impression that it is not necessary to practice scales in order to become a fine pianist. Of course, Mr. Hofmann doesn't practice scales. Why should he? He has already practiced them for forty years."

74

NO TIME FOR PRACTICE

Speaking of practicing, what is really sad is the fact that there are so many highly motivated and talented students who simply do not have the time for practice. These students are often detained after school each day for extra curricular events and do not get home until six or seven o'clock in the evening when it is time for dinner. After dinner they have many hours of homework.

These students are usually very bright and do well in school. They will often continue with piano lessons until the pressure gets too much for them. What these students lack, unfortunately, is strong parental guidance. Without this guidance, these highly motivated students will, time after time, take on more activities than they are capable of handling. It is the parents' responsibility to sit down with these students and decide just what is important and what is not important.

Today, parents seem to be under the impression that a child who practices soccer three times a week after school, goes to ballet class one day, an art class one day, religion class on Saturday morning, takes a piano lesson once a week and tops that off with a drama class, is being "well-rounded." The old adage, which is just as true today as it ever was, that these kids are becoming a jack-of-all-trades and master of none, seems to have been entirely forgotten.

Of course, many parents are going to ask, "What can I do to motivate a child who does not like to practice."

There is only one response that can be given to that question. Insist that the child practice. A job well done is the best possible motivator a child can have; the only way to get that job well done is through practicing. Students must be forewarned, however, to form good practice habits. It is a fallacy that practice makes perfect. Practice makes permanent.

75

CRITICS

Although musicians can be quite generous with their praises for another musician, they can be notoriously sarcastic when they feel that one is not worthy of praise. This is amply revealed in an old joke which many piano students are fond of quoting, substituting the name of John Doe with the name of the pianist to whom they refer:

"When he gives his debut the only thing the critics will have to say is, John Doe gave his debut last night. Why?"

But, jokes aside, sometimes even the finest of critics can come to the wrong conclusions. There was a student at the Los Angeles Conservatory who tells the story about Madam Lhevinne, who happened to be giving a six-week master class at the Conservatory. This student says that Madam Lhevinne happened to be passing the studio where he practiced and heard a Polonaise being played. She remained standing outside the room until the playing stopped and then entered the studio and began to berate him for such sloppy playing. She suggested several ways he could improve on that very popular Chopin selection.

That student claims he didn't have the heart to tell Madam Lhevinne that he only played the trumpet and that she had been listening to a recording of Jose Iturbi.

Well, Madam Lhevinne may have mistakenly assumed that it was a student playing, but she certainly was not mistaken in her assessment of the performance. Anyone having access to the recordings of Jose Iturbi and those of Josef Lhevinne performing that Polonaise are in for quite a shock when those recordings are played, one after the other. The first time I heard the Iturbi recording, after having listened to the Lhevinne recording, I thought for sure that my record player was on the blink.

Another rather amusing criticism occurred that same summer when Madam Lhevinne was at the conservatory. A former student of hers came out to the coast to study with her and the dean of the Conservatory asked me if they could rent my apartment for a few hours each day for this student to practice. Since I spent most of the day at the conservatory, I agreed. My apartment was actually in a professional building and there would have been no grounds for any complaints. There were students and teachers living in that building who practiced and taught from seven o'clock in the morning until eleven o'clock in the evening.

Well, during the second week while this student was practicing, a note slid under the door. My upstairs neighbor had written, "Please tell your teacher that you are wasting your time. My husband and I live upstairs and we have been listening to you practicing. You simply do not have what it takes to be a fine pianist. Do yourself a favor and get into another field before it is too late. I teach violin and my husband teaches piano. We have been teaching for many years and, believe me, we know talent when we hear it. But don't feel badly, dear, someday I'm sure you will thank us for this advice."

Now that doesn't seem very amusing; but it truly was. We all got a big laugh out of that note at the Conservatory. You see, the student who was practicing in my apartment was a young man in his late twenties or early thirties, who was already established as one of the finest accompanists in the United

States, as well as in Europe. He had also received rave reviews from the critics in every city in which he had given a solo recital. He had toured many countries as an accompanist with some of the top stars from the Metropolitan, including Rose Bampton and Risa Stevens. His name was Brooks Smith.

76

MISTAKEN IDENTITY

In our system of criminal justice, we often rely upon witnesses; but the value of that procedure should, at least, be questioned. Let me give you an example of the reliability of witnesses.

A few years ago, I attended the annual convention of the Music Teachers' Association of California which was held in San Jose. One evening, one of the guest "Artists" gave a grand performance in a two-hour recital. After the recital, another teacher and I were standing in the lobby of the hotel in which the convention was being held. Four or five teachers approached me and showered me with praise for my performance.

Now, the truth is that I resembled the performer just about as much as a hippopotamus resembles a gazelle; yet, this group of teachers had mistaken me for the pianist who had just performed, in spite of the fact they had been sitting no more than a few feet away from this performer and observing him for the past two hours.

The teacher with whom I had been chatting simply smiled as I turned to those admirers and said, "Thank you very much. I'm very happy that you enjoyed the program."

They were very pleased that they had been able to meet the "Artist." Why should I have taken that pleasure away from them?

Can we be certain that most witnesses are more reliable?

77

"EVERYONE, EXCEPT ME AND THEE"

If you're from back East, you've probably heard the Pennsylvania Dutch saying, "Sometimes, me thinks the whole world is queer, except me and thee, and, sometimes, I have me doubts about thee."

Well, according to a reviewer in the August 10th, 1993 edition of the New York Magazine in reviewing a recent biography of Benjamin Britten by Humphrey Carpenter, we can now add another "gay" to our list of composers.

Although this reviewer gives the book high praise, stating that it is elegantly written and an enthralling piece of work, I must state that I found the book utterly boring. True, as the reviewer states, Britten's acquaintances were numerous, reading like a page from "Who's Who" amongst musicians, artists, writers, poets, and painters. If, as the reviewer states, these characters come alive at the hands of Humphrey Carpenter, they must be members of the walking dead. Mr. Carpenter's writing is straight out of dullsville. A head full of facts he may have; but a Catherine Drinker Bowen or an Alexander Poznansky he ain't. No doubt, at the hands of another author, a biography of Britten could be quite entertaining.

The reviewer ends his review by mentioning some of America's noted composers, who, like Benjamin Britten, happened to be homosexuals: Samuel Barber, Aaron Copland, Virgil Thompson, Leonard Bernstein, John Cage, Charles T. Griffes, Marc Blitzstein, Ned Rorem, John Corigliano, William Flanagan, David Diamond, and Henry Cowel.

Reminds me of another book I read, by Harry Hay, in which he speaks of Richard Buhlig as being "gay." I could have dropped my teeth since I had studied with Mr. Buhlig for over a year, back in the late forties, and I had not the slightest inkling that he was a homosexual. Of course, I was quite young, just out of the service and very naïve. Had I known, let me assure anyone who might think otherwise, my respect and high regards towards that great master of the keyboard would not have been diminished. As attested by Harold Schonberg of the New York Times and author of "The Great Pianist," Mr. Buhlig was a great pianist and an outstanding teacher.

78

TWO PIANOS IN D MAJOR (?)

I take a certain amount of umbrage ... don't you love that word "Umbrage?" It means that I am pissed off but it sounds much better ... at the rather flippant editorial in the San Francisco Examiner on October 20, 1993, concerning a recent study done at the University of California at Irvine. This study found that listening to the Music of Mozart has a positive effect on the brain.

The editorial states, "We've heard of mood music, but music as brain fuel raises questions." It then proposes a group of asinine questions, "If you play it louder, does it help? Are Mozart booster shots in order? Does the title of the sonata matter?"

The editorial states, "Scientists at Irvine say students who listened to Mozart's Sonata on Two Pianos in D Major scored higher on spatial reasoning tests. Unfortunately the elevated IQs only last for 10 minutes." Really? If so, these scientists need a little enlightening. Mozart composed a Sonata in D Major for Two Pianos. The Sonata is in D Major, not the two pianos. I'm inclined, however, to think this was just another blunder on the part of the editorial.

My main objection to this editorial is that the Examiner has done its readers an extreme disservice by dismissing this research so lightly instead of doing some investigation of, and reporting on, the many researches that have been done by several universities as to the positive effect classical music has on the brain.

The editorial ends with, "Finally, does Mozart guarantee results or will students still have to study? This whole thing might just be a lot of classical gas."

Indeed! It might take only a little research to discover that the editor of this piece of nonsense is the one who is full of gas.

79

MORE ABOUT MARIAN ANDERSON AND THE DAR

A while back, I wrote about having read about the DAR refusing to allow Marian Anderson the use of Constitution Hall for a concert in Washington, D.C.

Recently Dear Abby reported having received a letter from a spokeswoman from the DAR claiming that the DAR had not allowed Marian Anderson the use of the hall because it had already been booked for the night of the concert.

B.S. If such a story had any validity, kindly tell me why Eleanor Roosevelt was so incensed by the DAR's action that she resigned from the DAR because of this refusal.

That spokeswoman should wake up and smell the coffee. One would have to be terribly gullible, historically ignorant, naïve, or downright stupid to believe that the DAR refused the use of Constitution Hall for any reason other than the fact that Marian Anderson was black.

80

LEONARD BERNSTEIN

Soon after I started this journal, I wrote a short comment on a biography of Leonard Bernstein. To my way of thinking I felt that the author dealt more with the sensationalism of Mr. Bernstein's escapades between the sheets than his other attributes.

Now, along comes another biography of Leonard Bernstein, by Humphrey Burton, a British TV Director who worked for years with Mr. Bernstein. According to the critics, this is a superb new biography, richly detailed and in-depth, and I would certainly agree. By incorporating hundreds of interviews with family, friends and colleagues, as well as having access to Bernstein's own rich legacy of papers and letters, Mr. Burton manages to reveal Maestro Bernstein as he has never been seen before.

Although I have just begun to read this biography, I find it readily apparent that Humphrey Burton is not Humphrey Carpenter. Thank God! In spite of the fact that they share a first name, Mr. Burton's style of writing is quite enjoyable. After all of these many, many months, I have still been unable to plow through Mr. Carpenter's biography of Benjamin Britten. Mr. Burton, on the other hand, keeps me turning the pages and I am fairly certain that the end will come all too soon.

81

DAVID BARBER'S OPERA HISTORY

On the cover Anna Russell is quoted as having said, "Why is it that people who write about classical music usually tend to be either desperately dreary or insufferably pompous? That's why it was such a joy to come across 'When the Fat Lady Sings' by David Barber. It brightened up my weekend no end."

Well, while I was browsing through books on music, a few days ago, I picked up this delightful book, subtitled "Opera History As It Ought To Be Taught" and I would encourage anyone to read it if they would like to be amused while picking up a bit of opera history without having to read through all the boring parts.

Mr. Barber is a very clever writer who manages to supply the reader with an abundance of facts through his wit and humor.

If you're a fast reader, you'll probably get through "When The Fat Lady Sings" in less than an hour; but, I'd be willing to bet you'll spend much more time re-reading and quoting from this most enjoyable treatise.

82

AND, OPERA IN A NUTSHELL

Just picked up what I would call a marvelous companion to Mr. Barber's "When The Fat Lady Sings." A book by Roger England, entitled "Opera—What's All The Screaming About." Well, the book, itself, is a scream. Just out in paperback, this is one great book about opera. It is packed with enjoyable facts about opera.

As the cover says, this entertaining guide to opera will hook its readers by the first chapter that summarizes the plots of fifty popular operas in outrageous, yet accurate, tabloid headlines.

Pick up a copy of this ever-delightful book and read, laugh and learn.

83

TIME TO LET HOROWITZ REST IN PEACE

Fans of Vladimir Horowitz will be enraptured by the book "Remembering Horowitz," compiled and edited by David Dubal, in which 125 leading concert pianists such as Emanual Ax, Lazar Berman, Shura Cherkassky, Van Cliburn, Rudolf Firkusny, Gary Graffman, Grant Johannesen, Alicia de Larrocha, Maurizzio Pollini, Charles Rosen, Peter Serkin, and 114 others have written ecstatic reviews of their impressions of Horowitz.

Unfortunately, after reading through about 50 of these short essays, one gets the feeling that one is listening to a broken record. The hyperbole all too often becomes too saccharine.

However, in my opinion, in addition to the interview on CD with Mr. Horowitz, the most outstanding feature of this book is the short biographical sketches which Mr. Dubal has supplied us with before each of the pianists' essays. These sketches, as well as being a relief from the repetitive "I love Horowitz" theme which permeates these essays, makes this book more than a welcome edition to anyone's library.

Throughout this journal, I have mentioned Horowitz several times; so, now I think it is time to let him rest in peace.

84

MORE ABOUT GOTTSCHALK

As editor of the monthly News Letter for the San Mateo County, California Branch of the Music Teachers' Association, the following bit of information about Louis Moreau Gottschalk was provided in answer to the Trivia Question: "Who was America's first super-star?"

Gottschalk was born in New Orleans on May 8, 1829. He was the first American-born pianist and composer to become internationally famous, the first to use in his compositions the indigenous folk melodies and rhythms of the New World and America's first "Piano Super-Star."

In 1842 he was sent to France where he studied with Berlioz. He met Chopin who said, "My child, I predict that you will become the king of pianists."

While still in his teens, Gottschalk brought forth a series of compositions based on his memories of Creole and Negro melodies. France acclaimed these compositions as it had acclaimed Chopin's mazurkas and polonaises. His performances created a sensation all over Europe and when he returned to the United States he became even more of a sensation. It is said that he gave more than 80 concerts in New York alone during the 1855-6 season. He was the musical sensation of the time and stories told of swooning young ladies were legend and rivaled those told of Franz Liszt.

Writing in his diary, in 1862, Gottschalk said, "I have given eighty-five concerts in four months. I have traveled fifteen thousand miles on the railroad. In St. Louis I have seven concerts in six days; in Chicago - five in four days. A few more weeks in this way and I should become an idiot."

In April 1865, Gottschalk left for a tour of the West and from California he sailed to South America where he gave concerts in Peru, Bolivia, Chile, Argentina and Brazil, being hailed in the latter country as a monarch of music. It was in Brazil, however, that he contacted yellow fever and died on December 18, 1869.

Incidentally, one might wish to note that before going to study with Berlioz, Gottschalk was refused admission to the Paris Conservatory. The director, without as much as an interview or an audition, dismissed him, claiming that "America could produce nothing but steam engines."

The above was written in the September, 1994 issue of the aforementioned newsletter. Sometime in December of that same year, I was pleasantly surprised to find that Frederick Starr's "Bamboula, The Life and Times of Louis Moreau Gottschalk" had come out just in time for me to report it in the January, 1995, issue of the newsletter, with the following comment:

I'm sorry to say that I did not discover S. Frederick Starr's "Bamboula, The Life and Times of Louis Moreau Gottschalk," in time to report it in the December News Letter. This new biography of Gottschalk is truly one that should be on the shelves of every music teacher in the country. It is a well-written, superb, well-researched biography of the fabulous Louis Moreau Gottschalk, America's first great pianist. Indeed, as Harold C. Schonberg reports, "Mr. Starr brings the man and his period vividly to life."

William Ferris, Director, Center for the Study of Southern Culture at The University of Mississippi, says, "This long awaited biography of Louis Moreau Gottschalk is a classic study. Starr shapes an unforgettable portrait of America's first internationally recognized composer."

I have no doubt you will want to add it to your collection. Based on extensive research, including hundreds of letters written by Gottschalk which are used here for the first time, "Bamboula" illuminates an exotic but tragic life, as well as one of the most democratic phases of American cultural life, a world with impresarios and America's first bohemian circle. A major biography in every sense, "Bamboula" will help to re-establish Gottschalk's place in American musical history.

85

OLGA SAMAROFF STOKOWSKI

I was very pleasantly pleased the other day when I walked into a bookstore here in San Mateo and saw a book on display about the life and times of Olga Samaroff. The book was entitled "Olga Samaroff Samaroff Stokowski: An American Virtuoso on the World Stage" by Bonna Staley Kline. Although I had not known Madam Samaroff personally, I had, indeed, heard much about her being a very great teacher and pianist. One of my teachers had studied with her and Olga had, herself, been a student of Ernest Hutcheson with whom Helen Scoville had studied (see chapter 54 of this Journal).

Sitting down to browse through the book, I very soon realized that I must have it. Immediately when I returned home, I sat down to read; but, after the first couple of chapters, I was interrupted by students who had come for their lessons. I was, however, very much anxious to get back to Ms. Kline's book. I suppose another reason for my having been so intrigued with this account of Olga Samaroff is the fact that she, along with the Lhevinnes, were the very pillars of the piano faculty from the very inception of The Juilliard, until Olga's death in 1948.

In this book, Ms. Kline makes it quite clear that Olga Samaroff was also a pillar of information about the music world during her lifetime, having been on intimate terms with so many of the world's finest musicians and concert artists.

"Olga Samaroff Stokowski" is a highly readable and an enjoyable book. I believe it is a "Must Read" for any and all aspiring young pianists as well as for anyone who wants to know what it was like to be an eminent figure in the music world during the '20's, '30's, and '40's.

Before I end this section of my journal, I must say that I was somewhat surprised when I read that Olga did not approve of her students listening to recordings of compositions of which those students were learning. In my many years of teaching I have, of course, encountered other fine teachers who felt the same about not letting students listen to recordings; but I am thoroughly convinced that Madam Lhevinne's approach to this matter is much more enlightening. Olga Samaroff's approach was quite contrary to what Madam Lhevinne espoused when I was studying with her (see chapter 22 of this journal). But, I must hastily add that I got the impression, upon reading Ms. Kline's book that Madam Samaroff's approach to teaching almost totally coincided with that of Madam Lhevinne's.

Finally, I would also like to supply this tidbit of information: Remember my mentioning that Madam Lhevinne had told a story about a famous concert artist who challenged those who claimed that they could tell whether a man or a woman was playing by simply listening to the recording. Well, although Madam Lhevinne did not mention the artist by name (see chapter 22), now that I have read Ms. Kline's book, I am thoroughly convinced that the artist was none other than Olga Samaroff. Ms. Kline, as a matter of fact, describes this very episode in the life of Olga and I believe it would be highly unlikely that such a happening could have occurred twice.

86

DOCTOR OSTWALK AND GLENN GOULD

Those who are familiar with Dr. Ostwald's "Schumann the Inner Voices of a Musical Genius" will, no doubt, be thrilled with his latest and final work "Glen Gould The Ecstasy and Tragedy of Genius." I say final work because the Associated Press, on the 28th of May, 1996, reported on that day that Dr. Ostwald, a UC San Francisco psychiatry professor had died and that the biography of the Canadian pianist, Glenn Gould was scheduled for publication next year.

Well, this book came out in the summer of 1997 and I immediately purchased a copy. I must confess that I was unable to put the book down from the time I opened it and learned that Dr. Ostwald had met Glenn Gould after a concert in San Francisco on February 28, 1957, and became and remained friends, until the very last chapter wherein Dr. Ostwald describes the funeral service at Saint Paul's Anglican Church in Toronto, Canada.

Now I must make it quite clear that when I read Dr. Ostwald's "Schumann the Inner Voices of a Music Genius," I was overwhelmed by the beauty and depth of the insight into the life of Schumann, his music as well as the very soul of that composer. His writing was clear and the documentation comprehensive. In that book, I felt that Dr. Ostwald actually let his reader listen to the inner voices of a musical genius. However, no doubt due to the fact that Glenn was a contemporary who lived in my own time, I found myself eagerly turning each page of this most exciting book about one of this century's most compelling artists.

As a psychiatrist, as well as a personal friend of Mr. Gould, Dr. Peter Ostwald sheds much light on the numerous eccentricities of Mr. Gould as well as reminding us of many of his charms. Much of the anecdotal material presented in this biography is delightful, even up to the very end when, as Dr. Ostwald tell us, that Glenn had the very last word as one could hear him humming along with the Aria from the Goldberg Variations which was played at his funeral.

To be sure, Mr. Gould, as well as Robert Schumann, was tragically disturbed and Dr. Ostwald has clearly defined these disturbances as well as leaving us with the unanswered question: Would the life of either of these musical geniuses been as fruitful had they not been so disturbed?

87

BERNSTEIN REVISITED

I can't say why I was interested in still another version of the life of Leonard Bernstein; there are two biographies already sitting on my shelves—one by Joan Peyser and one by Humphrey Burton. But soon to join them is a recently purchased volume by Meryle Secrest. I have admired Bernstein ever since he began bringing music to children on those weekly programs. In recent years, schools have done very little in this direction, since most programs, bands, orchestras, glee clubs and courses on music appreciation have been deleted from the curriculum, ostensibly, due to a lack of funding. As one of my colleagues put it, "There are funds but the priorities are not well thought out." He is convinced that all too large a part of the funds are spent on athletic activities. He refuses to refer to these activities as "sport," and often quotes a well-known endeavor to promote athletic activities as a commercial adventure that the word "sport" no longer applies. In the lower grades this activity is another required course. In higher grades it has become big business.

According to the hype expounded on the covers of each of the three biographies mentioned above is honest, revealing, fascinating and definitive. All three authors seem to agree that Mr. Bernstein's energy and his penchant for self-promotion far surpassed the norm. His sexual drive, according to these authors, was certainly not lacking either. Albeit that it was, it seems, often used to open doors. In reading Ms. Secrest's version, she makes it quite clear, even if she does so through the words of others, that bedding down with Dimitri Mitropoulos and Aaron Copland, was the key that opened doors. However, it is also quite clear, from all three authors, that his preference was for males of a more tender age. One should not read into this that Leonard was a pedophile, although that is the description one of his girl friends used when speaking to Koussevitzky. But that was not quite true. From all reports, those most likely to enamor Mr. Bernstein were handsome young men in their late teens or early twenties.

Of all three books, I believe Mr. Secrest was the most adept when supplying us with the "who, when and where" of some of these sexual exploits. One must, however, congratulate her on having a good sense of propriety in that the "what" and how was never once mentioned.

Anyone reading about Mr. Bernstein's final days might certainly come to the conclusion that he was HIV positive and suffered from AIDS; however there is absolutely no proof available that this was so and those close to him have been emphatic in their denials.

88

MARC BLITZSTEIN AND THE CRIME OF HATE

I must confess that I am totally unfamiliar with Marc Blitzstein and his music. However, in a biography of Leonard Bernstein, by Meryle Secrest, Mr. Blitzstein is mentioned several times. According to Ms. Secrest, Marc Blitzstein's Brechtian Opera, "The Cradle Will Rock," was first produced in 1937 and later, in 1939, a rather successful production was mounted by Leonard Bernstein and a classmate from Harvard. Afterward, this production, which was presented at the Sanders Theatre, Marc, Leonard and the cast members celebrated at an Italian restaurant on Harvard Square.

Down through the years Marc and Leonard remained good friends and Marc's sudden and tragic death was quite an emotional shock to Maestro Bernstein.

Before I tell you about Marc's sudden death, let me tell you about a movie I had watched on television just the night before I had read about Marc and his ill-fated trip to Martinique. This movie was a true story based on a real hate crime which had been reported in the news several months prior to the production of the movie. Perhaps you may recall the report that a "gay" sailor had been beaten to death by two of his shipmates, solely because the victim was a homosexual.

Now, back to Marc Blitzstein. Shortly after viewing that movie called "Another Mother's Son," I went back to reading Meryle Secrest's "Leonard Berstein." On page 304, Ms. Secrest related the circumstances surrounding the death of Marc. If you haven't guessed already, Marc was beaten, robbed and left for dead by three sailors while vacationing in Martinique in January 1964. Ms. Secrest does not tell us whether or not this was an actual "gay bashing." She does, however, say that Marc had picked up these three sailors, one from Martinique and two from Portugal, in a bar. After beating and robbing him, they left him for dead. He died the following day in the hospital.

Such "gay bashing" is not rare. Still, when they occur, we are prone to ask, "Why?" But would it be more truthful to ask, "Why not?"

These "gay bashers" are merely doing what they have been taught to do. Have they not been told that "Queers, faggots, fruits, pansies, perverts, etc., are not fit to live?" Have not fundamentalist preachers taught them that AIDS was brought upon by the wrath of God because they dared to love another human being who happened to be of the same sex? Have these preachers and their followers attended Gay Pride Parades carrying signs which read "God Hates Faggots." "Thank God for AIDS" and even "Kill a Queer for Christ?"

So, "Why not, indeed?"

89

MORE ABOUT THAT TCHAIKOVSKY RUMOR

The subtitle to this entry into my memoirs could very well be "Here We Go Again," by Anthony Holden. Mr. Holden goes to great lengths to dispute Alexander Pozansky's contention that the rumor about the death of Tchaikovsky being a suicide was false.

Mr. Holden does supply us with quite a bit of what seems to be convincing evidence that the death of Tchaikovsky was a suicide. However, I am convinced that Mr. Poznansky's biography of, as well as his account of Tchaikovsky, is more reliable than that of Mr. Holden (see Chapters 54 and 69).

While I readily admit that Mr. Holden's views, as well as his state evidence, contain much of which to ponder, I am inclined to believe that Mr. Poznansky presents the better argument.

However, I would certainly ask that the many who are interested in the life of Tchaikovsky read both biographies before making up their minds about the validity of either views. Both authors have given us a superb account of the life of this musical genius. Both have a lot to say and both have said it well. Certainly no well-read musician should be without a copy of both of these biographies in his or her collection.

90

A CHANGE FOR THE BETTER

Needless to say, there have been numerous and vast improvements over the past few decades in the caliber of piano teachers, as well as in the ability of students to perform. Josef Lhevinne, in his booklet, "Piano Pedagogy," remarked that during the first half of the twentieth century, students entering The Julliard were ill-prepared, in spite of the fact that the majority of students accepted at this most prestigious institution were there on a scholarship. Unfortunately, Mr. Lhevinne reported that students were terribly remiss in their knowledge of key-board harmony, music history, technical facility, as well as their ability to sight-read music at even an intermediate level. Today, I believe that Mr. Lhevinne would be pleasantly surprised at the progress that has been made within the past few years. The caliber of teachers has greatly improved. Of course, there were fine teachers during the era of which Mr. Lhevinne speaks, but I believe most pedagogues would probably agree that they were few and far between; so many teachers lacked the formal training required to be a good performer or teacher and many who were good performers lacked the desire or the ability to teach.

For the past several years, as a member of the Music Teachers' Association of California, my experience as a teacher, as well as an evaluator of students who have enrolled in that organization's Certificate of Merit Program, has led me now to believe that there exists a plethora of very talented and well-trained pianists and teachers today. Long gone are the days when Johnnie studied with his aunt down the street who had a year or so lessons from a fairly well-known teacher and decided that she was ready to put up her sign and begin a class of her own. Occasionally, Johnnie's aunt continued to progress along with her students and eventually became fairly adept at her trade when teaching beginners but extremely inadequate when trying to teach beyond that level. Fortunately, the National Guild of Piano Teachers, as well as some state organizations, such as the California Music Teachers' Association, have done an almost miraculous job of raising piano teachers standards to a very high level, far beyond the standards hinted at by Josef Lhevinne in the early nineteen-twenties ("Basic Principles in Pianoforte Playing," first publication by Theodore Presser Company, Philadelphia, 1924).

91

ENOUGH, ALREADY!

Well, I suppose one could go on with a journal such as this forever; but I think there comes a time when we must say, "Enough already!"

So, since so many these days are making predictions, I would like to end this journal with a little prediction of my own:

"Someday, hopefully in the not too distant future, I predict that parents will come to the realization that their children will not learn to play the piano without practicing."

So! Whassamatta? I can dream, can't I?

92

A CODA

It was not my intention, when I first began these memoirs, to offer advice to teachers. Heaven knows, there is a plethora of more than excellent teachers throughout the country today who certainly need no advice from me. Never-the-less, a colleague of mine, who is also a member of the Music Teacher's Association of California, suggested that since I had studied with several renowned pedagogues, there might be more than a few teachers who would be interested in suggestions that some of these well-known teachers had to say.

After so many, many years, it is difficult for me to remember much of what went on in these classes; many things said, I'm certain, were said by more than one teacher but let me try to give the reader an over-all picture of a few points which I have tried to incorporate in my own teaching.

Let me start with Richard Buhlig. As a student of the Los Angeles Conservatory of Music and Arts, I was privileged to attend a class at the home of Mr. Buhlig every Wednesday morning for over a period of two years. Perhaps one of the things that I recall Mr. Buhlig stressing again and again, was the long musical phrase and that a student, in his words "should not give the impression that one is jumping over a fence at each bar-line." Of course, the rhythmical flow of beats should be felt but anything more than a very subtle slight stress is often not required on the first count of a measure. Mr. Buhlig also believed that no lesson was complete unless the student brought along either a selection by Bach or Scarlatti.

Earle Voorhies: While Mr. Voorhies had, I believe, studied, at least for a while, with Madam Lhevinne, as well as with Olga Samaroff, he told me that he was actually a pupil of Alexander Siloti when he was a student at The Juilliard in New York. Perhaps one of the most important features I recall Mr. Voorhies demonstrating was how to repeat a single note or a chord very rapidly. Unfortunately, I am unable to put this procedure into words; I truly believe it can only be explained by demonstration. However, another detail that I remember so well, and believe it is extremely important when teaching my students, is to insist that the student not only practice hands separately but that they practice each voice linearly through the entire piece. Various voices were then to be played simultaneously. The Chopin Prelude in C Minor (Op. 28, No. 20) is a marvelous selection to demonstrate this procedure and, as a matter of fact, the selection that Mr. Voorhies used at the time he brought this idea to my attention. Starting with the bass, play the octaves throughout the entire piece. Then play the very highest voice (call it the soprano) all the through the entire piece. Then do the same with the inner voices. After learning each voice, practice two of them (say the outer voices) simultaneously. Then, practice the inner voices separately, etc. Once you have learned to put all of the voices together, try to play all of the voices together but stressing a different voice as you play. The soprano (the melody line) or the bass (the lower line is easy but try one that is not so easy) and the alto (the voice just under the soprano). To be able to bring out any one of the inner voices while performing all of the other voices is an outstanding accomplishment, as well as being a great tool in teaching the student the importance of listening to separate voices.

Helen Scoville: Helen Scoville, for many years prior to becoming a faculty member of the Manhattan School of Music, was an assistant to the eminent concert artist and teacher, Ernest Hutcheson, at The Juilliard. She was also an internationally acknowledged concert artist. I am particularly indebted to Ms. Scoville for her uncanny ability to dissect my performance and suggest ways of improving it through various ways of practicing. Without a doubt, one of the most valuable lessons she regularly imparted was the importance of gaining speed by practicing slowly. Let's, for example, take another Chopin prelude, the one in G (Op. 28, No. 3). Practice each measure separately but (and this is very important) end on the first note of the next measure. By over-lapping any tendency to hesitate can be avoided. Now, begin practicing counting, very slowly, four counts to each group of sixteenth-notes. Do this four times (stop on the first note of the next measure but continue to cunt up to four to give the muscles of your fingers a rest). Next, practice the same measure, continuing to count up to four but playing two-sixteenth notes to each count (the tempo should be exactly double the tempo you used when counting one sixteenth-note to a count). After repeating this, double the tempo (four sixteenth-notes to a count). If one finds they are unable to perform the measure at this suggested tempo then, according to Ms. Scoville, he or she, should begin the whole process over, one count per sixteenth-note but slower than previously. The goal, of course, is to continue the whole process without changing tempo. The final round would be the tempo in which you wish to perform the entire selection.

Finally, Madame Lhevinne: Surely, no one needs an introduction to Rosina Lhevinne, always referred to as "Madam Lhevinne" by her students. Throughout my memoirs, I have often mentioned Madame Lhevinne. Anyone having the good fortune to have studied with this great teacher, as well as a great human being, will, without a doubt, remember that she insisted upon absolute technical perfection. And to her, perfection meant to perform the music as near as possible to what the composer intended, by observing, listening and above all else, making the piano sing. "Listen, listen! Sing, sing! Make the piano sing!" were the words she must have repeated millions of times during her long, long career as a teacher. Rarely, if my lessons with her were typical, and I believe they were, did she hear technical studies. It was, to a great extent, preordained that one's technique had already been developed to the highest level prior to having begun to study with her. To an aspiring artist whose technical qualifications did not meet her exacting demands, a lesson with her could be quite frustrating. I've seen many a student burst out in tears as they strived, again and again, to adjust to her demands. Such tears came not from any harshness on the part of Madam Lhevinne but out of being unable to live up to Madam Lhevinne's expectations, which would, more often than not, require an almost endless amount of practice before one could reach that goal. Although Madame Lhevinne primarily insisted that one pay close attention to the score, using the urtext if at all possible, she often suggested that one practice the scales, using the standard fingering but being able to start on any note within a scale with the proper finger. For example, if one were to start a C Major scale on the key of "E," then one would start with the third finger in both hands and then proceed to use the correct fingering for that scale. Also, she highly recommended that one practice the Hanon studies (The first twenty exercises to be performed in all keys) as well as Plaidy exercises (particularly the studies in double thirds and double sixths). Some of her pet peeves were students who neglected the proper performance of slurs. The end of the slur was to be played softer than the note or notes beginning a slur and never, never to be "bumped" off at the end, regardless of whether there might be a dot (staccato) at the end of the slur. She expected a student to play "legato" without the benefit of the pedal. The pedal was to be used to enhance the music. "Fingers," according to Madam Lhevinne were to be glued to the keys. "Walking from one finger to the next" and "holding on to the keys as one would do if clinging to the edge of a cliff." I also remember her stating that she had long gotten over being surprised that so few students ever learned the proper execution of the three types of staccato marks: The dot, the wedge and the dot under a slur or line. She said when a student plays a staccato improperly, she simply referred them to Joseph Lhevinne's small booklet on the principles of pianoforte playing published by

Dover Publications. Finally, Madam Lhevinne, in spite of the fact the overwhelming majority of her students aspired toward a concert career, she often expressed her profound wish that students study music as an avocation. "If a vocation in music is the result, it is fine, but the primary goal should be directed toward an avocation. Regardless, the finest training and the finest teacher should be insisted upon. Progress is stimulation and the more one progresses, the more enjoyment one will obtain. Not much joy will come from no progress. One should consider music as a vocation only when one is completely and thoroughly convinced that he or she would never be happy in any other field."

However, if one wanted music as a vocation, Madam Lhevinne had the following suggestions when practicing:

— Examine the score carefully.
— Practice a small section at a time, preferably a phrase, but overlap by stopping on the first beat of the next phrase.
— Practice ever so slowly at first, hands separately if needed, in order to make certain no mistakes are made (she said that Joseph Lhevinne always recommended that a phrase wherein a mistake occurred should be practiced at least sixteen times for each time the mistake was played).
— Although many repetitions may be required before a phrase is completely learned, one should always listen carefully, always trying to improve the phrase with each repetition and not just repeating it mechanically.
— If at all possible, practice the same time each day. A good rule of thumb is to not practice more than two hours at a time without a break. If you get tired, lie flat on your back on the floor for fifteen or twenty minutes, making every effort to remove all thoughts from your mind and rest.
— Above all else, even when practicing scales or other exercises, make the piano sing.

J.B.

ABOUT THE AUTHOR

In 1946, shortly after having returned from the South Pacific where he served the last two years of his three years in the Army, Jim Barnhart entered the Los Angeles Conservatory of Music. He became a faculty member of that conservatory in 1948 and remained teaching there until he went to New York to continue his studies.

After more than twenty years as a teacher in a private studio in New York, Mr. Barnhart returned to California. Not long after returning to California, he was approached by a member of the California Music Teachers' Association suggesting that he become a member of that organization. Almost simultaneously upon becoming a member of the MTAC, he began to jot down a log of memories which eventually was given the name of "A PIANO TEACHER'S KALEIDOSCOPIC MEMORIES."

Mr. Barnhart has had the privilege of having studied with some of the world's most renowned teachers, including Earle C. Voorhies & Richard Buhlig at the Lost Angeles Conservatory of Music, Helen Scoville of the Manhattan School of Music and Rosina Lhevinne of The Juilliard School in New York.

BVG